"Lee Cohn, co-author of the essential *A Practical Handbook for the Actor*, has now written an equally important book exploring the director's process in working with actors. Cohn cuts straight through the nonsense which too often pollutes the Director-Actor relationship, and provides clear, concise, and practical tools toward the cultivation of stellar, effective performances – the heart-and-soul of any drama. Reminding us that acting choices must always serve the story, he provides directors with a workable framework for script analysis, rehearsal preparation, performance vocabulary, and real-time direction designed to ensure exciting results. In simple, straightforward prose, Cohn demystifies the process, and offers a cogent roadmap for navigating any directorial endeavor. *Directing Actors: A Practical Aesthetics Approach* is a must-read for both beginning directors and seasoned professionals, and serves as a valuable addition to the exploration of this too-often slippery topic."

Dr. Michael Peter Bolus, PhD, *Liberal Arts Department Chair, Los Angeles Film School; author; actor,* My Name is Dolomite

"*Directing Actors: A Practical Aesthetics Approach* is a must read for directors in film, television, and theater. A clear and concise breakdown of how best to use active language when directing actors. Refreshingly 'no nonsense' and to the point – Lee Cohn explains exactly how to get the most from your actors and craft grounded and truthful performances. Truly invaluable."

Maggie Kiley, *director,* Dirty John: The Betty Broderick Story, American Horror Story, Riverdale, and The Chilling Adventures of Sabrina

"Lee Cohn's frank and logical methods for directors working with actors should be required reading for anyone who plans to direct theater, film, or television. Finally, a clear-cut guide for those entering the realm of directing."

John Putch, *veteran film and TV director,* Scrubs, Cougar Town, My Name is Earl, Poseidon Adventure, and American Pie Presents: The Book of Love

"For anyone interested in theater, reading Lee Cohn's book on directing is like having a private conversation with a brilliant director. This remarkable book considers the director as interpreter of the script as well as collaborator with every artist involved in the production. The advice is practical, doable, and fun. It is a candid roadmap for how a production moves from the page to the stage, and everyone – directors, playwrights, actors, designers, audiences, and even producers – will learn from it."

Evangeline Morphos, *producer; Professor, Columbia University (retired)*

"Many moons ago Lee Cohn decided to write a book with a few of our NYU classmates entitled *A Practical Handbook for the Actor*. Over the years I have either gifted or recommended said book to actors young and old. Lee's teachings have always been one of the sharpest and most necessary blades I carry as an actor. Mr. Cohn now gifts us with his solo effort. Read it and watch your talent grow before your eyes! Buy this book! If you can't afford it, steal it!"

Titus Welliver, *star of* Bosch, Gone Baby Gone, and Deadwood

"Lee excels at stripping away the nonsense and delivering a set of practical tools that will help any director take their craft to the next level. If you're a director, or thinking of becoming one, then you should buy this book. I was lucky enough to have Lee as my teacher. And now, thanks to this book, you can too. Lee's writing is clear, concise, and absolutely crucial for up-and-coming directors."

Jeffrey Addiss, *Emmy-winning writer-producer,* The Dark Crystal: Age of Resistance

Directing Actors

Directing Actors: A Practical Aesthetics Approach is the first book to apply the Practical Aesthetics acting technique to the craft of directing.

Lee Cohn lays out a step-by-step, no-nonsense methodology for the director that includes a deep dive into the mechanics of storytelling, the rehearsal process, working with writers, and the practical realities of the director's job. Featuring end-of-chapter exercises, this book provides a clear and effective means of breaking down a script in order to tell a story with clarity, simplicity, and dramatic force and gives directors a clear working vocabulary that will allow effective communication with actors. The techniques in this book are applicable to any theatrical style and any media platform in which a director might work. Written in an accessible, conversational style, this book strips the process of directing down to its most essential components to explain how to become an "actor's director."

A must-read for students in directing courses and professional directors working with actors who prescribe to the Practical Aesthetics technique, as well as anyone interested in the process of working with actors, *Directing Actors* will help directors to get the very best their actors are capable of while approaching the work with a joyful, open spirit.

Lee Michael Cohn, MFA, is an internationally acclaimed, award-winning educator, writer, director, and filmmaker. He directed *Inside Private Lives (IPL)*, the hit show that was an *LA Weekly* Pick of the Week, was recommended twice by the *LA Times*, and received a rave review in *The New York Times*. IPL also placed in the top ten out of over 2,000 shows at the Edinburgh Theatre Festival. Lee is the co-author of *A Practical Handbook for the Actor*, a best-selling acting textbook (over 330,000 copies sold) that is required reading in hundreds of theatre programs all over the world. He lives in Los Angeles, but please don't hold that against him.

Directing Actors
A Practical Aesthetics Approach

Lee Michael Cohn

NEW YORK AND LONDON

First published 2021
by Routledge
605 Third Avenue, New York, NY 10158

and by Routledge
2 Park Square, Milton Park, Abingdon, Oxon, OX14 4RN

Routledge is an imprint of the Taylor & Francis Group, an informa business

© 2021 Lee Michael Cohn

The right of Lee Michael Cohn to be identified as author of this work has been asserted by him in accordance with sections 77 and 78 of the Copyright, Designs and Patents Act 1988.

All rights reserved. No part of this book may be reprinted or reproduced or utilised in any form or by any electronic, mechanical, or other means, now known or hereafter invented, including photocopying and recording, or in any information storage or retrieval system, without permission in writing from the publishers.

Trademark notice: Product or corporate names may be trademarks or registered trademarks, and are used only for identification and explanation without intent to infringe.

Library of Congress Cataloging-in-Publication Data
Names: Cohn, Lee Michael, author.
Title: Directing actors : a practical aesthetics approach / Lee Michael Cohn.
Description: New York, NY : Routledge, 2021. | Includes bibliographical references and index.
Identifiers: LCCN 2020057186 (print) | LCCN 2020057187 (ebook) | ISBN 9780367547264 (hardback) | ISBN 9780367548452 (paperback) | ISBN 9781003090991 (ebook)
Subjects: LCSH: Theater—Production and direction. | Acting. | Theater rehearsals. | Aesthetics.
Classification: LCC PN2053 .C59 2021 (print) | LCC PN2053 (ebook) | DDC 792.02/8—dc23
LC record available at https://lccn.loc.gov/2020057186
LC ebook record available at https://lccn.loc.gov/2020057187

ISBN: 978-0-367-54726-4 (hbk)
ISBN: 978-0-367-54845-2 (pbk)
ISBN: 978-1-003-09099-1 (ebk)

Typeset in Adobe Caslon Pro
by Apex CoVantage, LLC

This book is dedicated to my daughters, Danielle ("Don't mention the war") and Ava ("Git 'er done") Cohn.
You are the very air that I breathe.

Contents

ACKNOWLEDGMENTS   XI
AUTHOR'S NOTE   XIII

PART I
Preparation   1

1   Introduction   3

2   The Director and the Text   9

3   Actions   32

4   Practical Aesthetics Script Analysis   46

5   Through-Line Analysis   71

6   The Director's Notebook   80

PART II
The Rehearsal Process   101

7   Early Rehearsals   103

Contents

8 Blocking the Scene — 118
9 Adjustments and Run Throughs — 143
10 Comedy: The Serious Business of Humor — 152
11 Conclusion — 181

Suggested Reading and Viewing — 185
Index — 190

Acknowledgments

I would like to thank the following awesome humans in alphabetical order:

Lucia Accorsi the most patient and supportive editor any writer could wish for. Thanks for letting me leave in the jokes.

Melissa Bruder, Madeleine Olnek, Nathaniel Pollack, Robert Previto, and Scott Zigler – my co-authors of *A Practical Handbook for the Actor*. We helped start a revolution in the theatre – not bad for six kids in jeans and t-shirts.

Zach Calhoun for the use of an excerpt of his interview with Leonora Gershman-Pitts.

Ava Cohn for her terrific visual ideas.

Danielle Cohn for her great suggestions, sharp eye for detail, and catching all the typos that I missed. Thanks, Bean!

The megatalented Debra Diament for allowing me to use the lyrics from her song "Chocolate and Strawberries." (Check out her old band – The Januaries – you won't be sorry.)

Jeff Eyres, my partner in many crimes, for his feedback and eternal patience. I'm *sayin'*, bro.

My family!

Kate Fornadel and her team for their great work in preparing this manuscript for publication.

Tod Goldberg for his crash course in the realities of publishing a book in 2021.

Legal eagle Stacey Haber for her help with clearances. More than chow fun noodles from Wo Hop!

David Mamet for his support and for teaching me so many useful and important things a million years ago that I have never forgotten.

Robert McKee for allowing me to quote him.

My ninjutsu brothers and sisters – teachers, dojo-mates, and everyone who contributed to my advancement in the art. Ninpo Ikkan!

William Rabkin, writer and professor extraordinaire, for allowing me to quote him.

Dr. Morgaan Sinclair for her incredible insights on mythology, Jung, and Freud.

And last, but by no means least. . . Stacey Walker for championing this book and getting it in the door.

Author's Note

Whatever the medium – live theatre, film, television, or the latest technological marvel beaming content directly into our brains via computer, cellphone, or micro-implants – good acting is good acting, and the director's job regarding actors is pretty much the same.

This book is intended to lay out a useful, practical approach to help directors gain a deep understanding of the text and then, based on that understanding, give the actors simple, clear, and helpful instructions. You'll find many examples throughout the book taken from theatre, film, and television; the default medium is theatre, but please remember that the techniques and processes outlined herein are universally applicable. It's tiresome to write, and even more tiresome to read, constant reminders and references to every format with every example in the book. When appropriate to differentiate the needs of a particular format, I will do so, but in the main, everything in this book is adaptable to whatever medium you are working in.

Working with actors is great fun and very rewarding. I hope this book helps you achieve your creative goals with clarity and joy.

Lee Michael Cohn
Los Angeles, CA
2020

Part I
Preparation

1
INTRODUCTION

Thanks for checking out this book. It is my hope that you find it useful, hopefully as a cut-to-the chase guide to directing actors that will save you a lot of wasted time and energy and keep your therapy bills to a minimum. Time is your most precious commodity, and I hope this book helps you use it wisely.

So, let me answer the question that you're going to ask at some point, if you haven't done so already: *do we really need another book on directing?*

At the risk of sounding a tad immodest, I think maybe we do. At the very least, as the members of my tribe are wont to say, "Couldn't hurt."

There are a lot of very good books on directing, many of which have been in print for decades. Not to knock my predecessors – we all stand, in some way, on the shoulders of giants – but many books on the craft lean far too heavily on a theoretical/academic approach, and thus, the process often becomes complicated, cumbersome, and most importantly, *impractical*.

Actors are, in the main, very smart people; if directors lay a bunch of useless crap on them in rehearsal, they will usually nod politely (nobody wants to get fired), say something like "I see what you mean," and then, finding the direction to be vague, unhelpful, and beside the point, will go on about their business, doing the best they can to craft their performance in spite of the director's *unactable* instructions. So, we begin and end with the fundamental idea that any piece of direction must be doable in *real time*, within the physical reality of the scene. Seems like a simple concept, no? Then why do so many directors struggle to find a way to clearly articulate the behavior they require in a given scene and, further, to help the actors create it?

Most directors simply do not grasp the fundamental aspects of the actor's craft, a condition compounded by the fact that there are so many, often competing, schools of thought on how an actor should, you know, act. (A lot of those schools of thought are, by the way, utter nonsense, but that's a topic for another day.) Directors with a theatrical background tend to fare a bit better, but most young directors coming out of film schools have neither a deep understanding of nor a genuine appreciation for what an actor goes through. (If you really want to walk a mile or two in an actor's shoes, take an acting class. It will rock your world.) Great actors always make it look easy; I assure you, it isn't.

So how does a director communicate with actors quickly, efficiently, and effectively? In order to answer that question, which indeed forms the foundation of this book, the director needs to create a working vocabulary that *any* actor can process, whatever their training and experience, and that vocabulary must arise from an understanding of the mechanics of not only acting as a singular craft but how human beings process information.

The final arbiter of good direction begins with a simple question that must be constantly, relentlessly reiterated: *is this actable?* For the less experienced director, it's sometimes hard to draw that distinction; one's brilliant literary and psychological insights into a story and the characters who populate it do not necessarily help the actor when it comes down to the nuts and bolts of actually playing a scene, and sometimes those well-intended ideas actually prevent actors from doing their best work.

This book is loosely structured like the rehearsal process. You, the director, gets hired to direct a play. (Or a movie. Or a TV show. Or a whatever. Doesn't matter. The principles herein are universal.) Whoo hoo! So first, you need to break down the material so you are prepared to begin rehearsals. You need to understand every character's *intention*, every character's *relationship* to the other characters in each scene, and how each scene fits into the overall journey of the narrative. Then, you will sit day after day in a room with the actors, and it is your job to make sure that they supply the behavior necessary for each scene to function dramatically. *So, your understanding of the material informs every moment of the process, from the first table read to the final dress rehearsal.*

Here are a few first principles to bear in mind as you digest the information in this book:

1. *The story rules everything.* All direction to the actors, indeed all the choices made by a director, must serve the needs of the story. The director's preparation revolves around understanding the overall intent of the story and then parsing each scene into a dramatic conflict that serves that idea. (More on this. . . a lot more on this. . . to come.)
2. *The director must understand every character's intention in every scene.* If directors do not understand why each character is in a given scene and what they want, then they cannot direct the scene.
3. *Everything comes from action.* Everything – from what to tell the actors, to how to stage a scene, to costume choices – stems from the actions being pursued by the actors within the imaginary circumstances of the scene. *Everything.*
4. *Every scene must have a conflict.* Some scenes are more confrontational than others, but every scene must involve opposing forces fighting for what they want. Even in a poorly written scene, it's the director's job to tease out as much conflict as the scene will organically support.
5. *An actor can only perform an action.* All direction must ultimately be reduced to a simple, *playable* action, that is, the pursuit of a clearly defined goal. "To get a favor," "to offer an apology," and "to correct a false impression" are *common tasks* that an actor can actually perform. You can do any of them *right now*. Go ahead, give one a try. Now, actions like "to make the world a better place" or "to convert a clam into a seahorse" are not actable. Go on, knock yourself out. See what I mean?

Years ago, a teacher of mine put it like this: if you're moving into a new house, you can give the movers instructions like, "Be careful with the big mirror" or "Put the couch against the wall and the love seat by the window." They are simple and clear. But if you say something like "Please make me feel happy in my new home," the movers would probably stare at you like you're from another planet and try to get out of there as quickly as possible. Acting choices work the same way. They have to be doable *right now*, otherwise they are useless.

6. *An actor cannot perform a psychological or emotional state of being.* Any direction that asks the actor to portray a state of being will lead to self-consciousness and *indicating*. All bad acting can ultimately be reduced to indicating, which simply means that the actor is *showing* the audience what they think the character should be thinking and/or feeling. An actor's job is to *always* pursue a singular goal (action) in each scene, not to pretend to feel or think something. Don't ever ask an actor to "be" something; directions like "be happy," "be angry," or "be confused" will lead the actor to counterfeit behavior akin to their basic understanding of that particular state of being. Rather, tell the actor to *do* something. "Get a friend to wise up," "stand up to a bully," or "demand clarification" are much better ways to get the intended results from the actor because they are simple, outwardly directed tasks.

7. *Good direction is free of jargon.* Directors often get caught up in technical mumbo jumbo. Also, usually with the best of intentions, directors often try to speak to each actor specifically from the vantage point of that actor's training. This often creates a "Tower of Babel effect" wherein what makes sense and is useful to one actor may be complete nonsense to another. For instance, the use of sense memory or emotional memory might work well with Method actors but be completely counterproductive with an actor steeped in Practical Aesthetics or classical British theatre training. Part of the goal of this book is to help the director create, in essence, a universal language that any actor can easily process. (For my fellow *Star Wars* geeks, the directorial equivalent of Galactic Basic.)

8. *BE PREPARED!* The rehearsal process must always contain room for the birth of new ideas and happy accidents born of the actors' spontaneity. It's important to enter into each rehearsal with a spirit of openness and exploration, but the director *must* identify the nature of the conflict in the scene and have a clear idea of what each character wants from the other. If the director doesn't understand these things, they haven't done their job, and thus they are not ready to direct the scene. Now, as Hank Williams said, "The good Lord willin' and the creek don't rise," as a director watches a scene come to life, they might have an insight that will take things in a new direction. But the director MUST begin each rehearsal with a clear agenda and an understanding of the mechanics of each scene.

9. *Good direction is invisible.* I once directed a show that got numerous excellent reviews and went on to win a bunch of awards. I was not mentioned in many of the reviews, so naturally, my ego was a bit bruised. *I worked my butt off on this thing*, I thought. I wanted to see my name in print adjacent to superlatives like "genius," "brilliant," and "we ought to erect a statue in Mr. Cohn's honor." And then it finally occurred to me: the fact that I wasn't mentioned actually meant that I did a good job. If an audience is thinking about the direction – the actor's performances, staging, pacing, use of theatrical elements, you name it – you messed up, my friend. The seams are showing. The audience's attention should *always* be on the story. If they are thinking of your direction, however brilliant, it means that the audience is now aware of the artifice. They've stopped dreaming the dream of the play. They've stopped living vicariously through the characters. In short, they've checked out.

And finally. . .

10. *Don't be a jerk.* Treat the actors, and everyone else, with respect. Period. Be polite and keep your hands to yourself.

***

The great filmmaker Martin Scorsese once said that, despite his decades of experience and having made some of the greatest films in the history of cinema, the first day on set he is always plagued by the same thought: "I'll never finish this picture." Directing ANYTHING, from a major studio film to a play in a 50-seat black box, can feel like a Herculean task. A million details, a million decisions to make. I felt the same way when writing this book; the elation of having secured the contract with a big-deal publisher (thanks, guys!) quickly gave way to *What have I gotten myself into? I'll never finish this thing. What do I know, anyway? Help!*

So what do we do when faced with a huge, daunting, multifaceted undertaking? Divide it up into small, manageable chunks. One step at a time. So, just like actors must learn to focus exclusively on what's in front of them in a scene, so must the director learn to focus on what is necessary, step by step, to build and execute a framework that will elicit from the actors the very best that they are capable of. That's how we're gonna roll.

So let's do this.

2
THE DIRECTOR AND THE TEXT

Your job as the director is to make sure that every element in the production tells the story, simply and clearly. Because this book is devoted to working with actors, we will not focus too much on other, equally important aspects of directing, like working with scenic and lighting designers, editors, etc. But when it comes to making any and all aesthetic decisions, always remember: *the story is the boss*. So, before you can begin rehearsing your actors, you need to have a clear vision of the story you intend to tell.

But what, exactly, is a story? According to screenwriting guru (I hope he doesn't mind me calling him that) Robert McKee, "A story expresses how and why life changes." Sometimes life changes for the better, sometimes for the worse, but the great writer, through the main character's journey, explicates something universal about the nature of life within the confines of the specific dramatic world they have created.

I trained for years in an ancient Japanese martial art. We often used the Japanese terms *ura* and *omote*. Simple translation: back and front, which was an easy shortcut to reversing the positions involved in various techniques. But there was a deeper meaning that unfolded as I progressed in the art: *that which is seen, and that which is hidden*. Almost every technique had a hidden, more deadly component that the more advanced practitioner would eventually unlock. Stories work the same way; setting, time period, style, genre, even the characters and their goals are what's on the surface, but every great story has a deeper resonance to the human condition that goes beyond the plot, beyond the subject matter.

Is the plot the same thing as the story? The award-winning screenwriter, novelist, and film professor William Rabkin gives the following definition: *plot is what happens; story is what happens and what it means.*

Ura and *omote*. That which is seen – or in story terms, *stated* – and that which is *implied*, but not necessarily stated directly.

Here are a few examples from well-known films and plays:

- The PLOT of *Rocky* is about an underdog, washed-up fighter who gets a shot at the heavyweight title. The STORY is about a good-hearted soul whose life went bad and who is trying to regain his manhood and self-respect.
- The PLOT of *Chinatown* is about a private detective trying to solve a murder for a client. The STORY is about a man who attempts to reconcile a long-buried personal tragedy by exposing unspeakable evil.
- The PLOT of *The Wizard of Oz* is about Dorothy trying to get to Oz so the Wizard can send her home. The STORY is about a girl becoming a woman by facing down her greatest fears.
- The PLOT of John Ford's revisionist Western *The Searchers* is about Ethan Edwards' (John Wayne) obsessive quest to rescue a young white girl who was abducted at a young age by the Comanche Native American tribe. The STORY is about a man coming to terms with, and letting go of, a lifetime of prejudice and hatred.
- The PLOT of *Lawrence of Arabia* is about T.E. Lawrence's attempt to unite the forever squabbling Arab tribes against the Turks during World War I. The STORY is of a man's growing and troubling understanding of his own savage nature.
- The PLOT of *American Graffiti* is about a bunch of high school kids trying to have fun cruising on the last night of summer. The STORY is about accepting the fact that childhood must end and that growing up means moving on.
- The PLOT of Jordan Peele's horror film *Get Out* is about a young, African American man who discovers that his girlfriend's family

is part of a cult of wealthy, suburban white people that uses black people's bodies for horrifying purposes. The STORY is about how racism and oppression of African Americans by whites continues to this day and can be found anywhere.
- The PLOT of the Korean film *Parasite* is about a likeable family running an elaborate con on a rich family so they can all get jobs. The STORY is about desperate people at the very bottom of the socioeconomic spectrum who will do anything to level up and get a long-denied taste of the good life.
- The PLOT of August Wilson's Pulitzer Prize–winning play *Fences* is about a middle-aged man doing his best to provide for his family and find some satisfaction with his own life. The STORY is about a man who is ultimately so consumed by his bitterness and disappointment that he destroys his own life by alienating his friends and family.
- The PLOT of Arthur Miller's *Death of a Salesman* is about Willie Loman's struggle to make a success of himself and his ne'er-do-well sons, Biff and Happy. The STORY is about a young man (Biff) who finally rejects the bogus expectations that have been placed on him and decides to finally live life on his own terms. (NOTE: I take the position here that Biff is the protagonist of the story. Let's debate over a beer.)
- The PLOT of Steven Spielberg's film *Munich* is about a team of Israeli Mossad agents who methodically track down and kill the terrorists responsible for the murder of Israeli athletes during the 1972 Olympics. The STORY is about the effect that killing and revenge has on the human soul.

Now, you might very well have a different take on each of these films and plays – I hope you do! But what we are illustrating here is that, working in tandem with the formal mechanics of the plot, each of these stories has a larger point about some aspect of human nature.[1] Again, that point needn't be overstated, or indeed stated at all, for it to resonate with the audience. In fact, one of the tropes of good dramatic writing is to never beat the audience over the head with the theme (unless it's done as ironic commentary, *à la South Park*). To do so is tantamount to blackmailing the audience into a specific emotional reaction; it's heavy-handed, obvious, and insulting to their intelligence. Writers have a term for this kind of bad, overly declarative writing: "on the nose."

Good writers don't preach; they tell a story that allows audience members to engage on their own terms. As the legendary Hollywood producer Samuel Goldwyn once observed, "Pictures were made to entertain; if you want to send a message, call Western Union."

Quite often, scenes in which characters stop pursuing their intentions to talk about their feelings, give another character their life story, or self-consciously ponder the moral and spiritual implications of their present circumstances impede the forward momentum of the narrative in the name of giving the audience "information." To paraphrase writer-director David Mamet, the audience does not want information. They want *drama* – characters with a clear and specific goal who face mounting obstacles in their quest to achieve that desired end. Even when characters discuss their dilemmas, it must be *dramatic*.

In *Lawrence of Arabia*, for example, there is only one scene in the entire film where Lawrence verbally acknowledges his inner struggle. When speaking to General Allenby, he relates an incident the desert that has left him deeply troubled:

LAWRENCE: I killed two people, I mean two Arabs. One was a boy. That was yesterday. I led him into a quicksand. The other was a man. That was before Aqaba anyway. I had to execute him with my pistol. There was something about it I didn't like.
ALLENBY: Well, naturally.
LAWRENCE: No, something else.
ALLENBY: I see. Well that's all right. Let it be a warning.
LAWRENCE: No, something else.
ALLENBY: What then?
LAWRENCE: I enjoyed it.

The scene is powerful because we had previously watched Lawrence kill a man for whom he had risked his life to rescue from certain death. This scene gives the audience a new insight into the character, and it's just enough for us to reframe our perception of who Lawrence is. Although the scene is "thematic," it is presented organically as a part of the character's ordeal; Lawrence is *actively* trying to come to terms with what he has just experienced, which advances the narrative and deepens the audience's understanding of the character. The great dramatist Robert Bolt knew that this singular mention of Lawrence's growing inner dilemma would be enough.

Similarly, in *Chinatown*, private detective Jake Gittes' shadowy past is only hinted at, but we know as the story progresses that his need to solve the Mulwray murder is in fact the means by which he is attempting to exonerate a tragic episode from his past that, for all his current success, still haunts him. What exactly happened to Jake in *Chinatown* is hinted at, but never fully revealed. Screenwriter Robert Towne gives the audience just enough clues to pique their curiosity – whatever Jake went through was traumatic enough to cause him to suffer a nervous breakdown and leave the police force forever. In this particular story, that's all we need to know. Towne lets the *audience* decide what it all adds up to and what might've happened.

At this point, we must take note of the fact that the derivation of meaning in any work of art, especially narrative works, is a fluid and ever-changing construct. Times change, social mores change, and we change with them. But from time immemorial, people have processed stories through the lens of their own life experience. It's almost impossible to do otherwise. There's an old anecdote about a physician who went to see the original 1947 Broadway production of *A Streetcar Named Desire* starring Marlon Brando, Kim Hunter, and Jessica Tandy. At the very end of the over two-hour play, a kindly doctor enters to take Blanche DuBois away to a mental institution. He's literally on stage for 30 seconds. When asked how he liked the show, the physician said he thoroughly enjoyed it. When asked what it was about, he replied that the play was about a compassionate doctor who rescues a unfortunate woman who had lost her mind. Apocryphal or not, it illustrates the point.

The plot-story dynamic also applies to the way an *audience* processes a story. They generally root for protagonists to achieve their goals, but what they really care about is this: *who is the character becoming?* In *Rocky*, the hero essentially fails in his goal to win the world heavyweight boxing championship, but it is nonetheless an uplifting ending because Rocky retains his good nature and manages — by fighting a courageous fight against a formidable opponent — to regain his manhood and self-respect. Imagine, however, if Rocky had won the fight but, in the process, transformed into a callous, ruthless, narcissistic jagoff. The audience would have had a much different *emotional* relationship to that outcome.

Similarly, in *The Godfather* and *The Godfather Part II*, Michael Corleone's overall goal is to protect his family at all costs. Despite his desire to take the Corleones out of the crime underworld and turn them "legit," he resorts to lies, extortion, violence, and murder, even killing his own brother, Fredo. The end of *The Godfather Part II* finds Michael alone, a hollow shell of his former self. His failure to protect his family is not what the audience mourns; it's the loss of Michael's very soul.

The same personalization of a narrative certainly holds true for theatre artists. As society's values evolve, great plays are constantly being reexamined and reinterpreted. We can see this most profoundly in Shakespeare; *The Merchant of Venice* was originally intended as a comedy, with Shylock, the Jewish moneylender, as a grotesque villain and an object of scorn and derision. This original intent of that character would never fly today because it would play as an exercise in ugly racial stereotyping and anti-Semitism. So, over the centuries, Shylock has morphed into a character who is shunned and demeaned by his community (Venice, not his fellow Jews) and whose demand for the pound of flesh is often portrayed as an expression of his pent-up rage at his mistreatment.

SALARINO
Why, I am sure, if he forfeit, thou wilt not take
his flesh: what's that good for?

SHYLOCK
To bait fish withal: if it will feed nothing else,
it will feed my revenge. He hath disgraced me, and
hindered me half a million; laughed at my losses,
mocked at my gains, scorned my nation, thwarted my
bargains, cooled my friends, heated mine
enemies; and what's his reason? I am a Jew. Hath

not a Jew eyes? hath not a Jew hands, organs, dimensions, senses, affections, passions? fed with the same food, hurt with the same weapons, subject to the same diseases, healed by the same means, warmed and cooled by the same winter and summer, as a Christian is? If you prick us, do we not bleed? if you tickle us, do we not laugh? if you poison us, do we not die? and if you wrong us, shall we not revenge? If we are like you in the rest, we will resemble you in that. If a Jew wrong a Christian, what is his humility? Revenge. If a Christian wrong a Jew, what should his sufferance be by Christian example? Why, revenge. The villany you teach me, I will execute, and it shall go hard but I will better the instruction.

So, the changing times have had an undeniable influence on how Shylock has been interpreted over the years; indeed, the character has become emblematic of the anger felt by members of any marginalized and abused group, ethnic or otherwise. Even though this postmodern view may not have been what Shakespeare had in mind when he wrote the play, it still works, arguably better than the original version.

Why?

Great art speaks to universal themes, and those themes are always subject to individual interpretation. To quote the writer Anaïs Nin, "We don't see things as they are, we see them as we are."

It is a testament to the complexity and richness of Shakespeare's work that radically differing points of view can still serve the story. *Hamlet* has been played as everything from a tragic, tortured hero to a spoiled, punk kid who has to man up and take care of business. The same holds true with every other great character, from G.B. Shaw's Saint Joan, to Tennessee Williams' Stanley Kowalski, to Troy Maxon in *Fences*: there is no single interpretation engraved in stone for these characters or the theatrical worlds they inhabit. So, get your highlighter out. . . .

Whatever you're going to direct, you have to have a point of view.

What does the story mean *to you*? What do *you* want to portray to the audience? Why are you telling this story, other than needing the gig (a perfectly good answer, by the way)? And how does your vision intersect with, and support, the dramatist's intentions? To better understand these concepts, let's take the first of many looks at the actor's craft.

The notion of the playwright's intentions has been at the core of many acting methodologies, most notably Practical Aesthetics, the technique outlined in *A Practical Handbook for the Actor*. (Yeah, yeah, you got me, I co-wrote it. Available at all your finer bookstores, if there are any actually left.) When breaking down a scene using Practical Aesthetics, actors always spot-check their choices to make sure they are in line with something the playwright might have intended. Common sense and a bit of useful acting technique are the actor's primary tools when assessing whether or not the chosen action is somehow expressive of the dramatic intent of the scene, along with a basic respect for the written word. Let's take the climactic courtroom scene in Aaron Sorkin's *A Few Good Men* between defense attorney Daniel Kaffee (Tom Cruise) and US Marine Colonel Nathan Jessup (Jack Nicholson). ("You can't HANDLE the truth!")

Kaffee is at his wit's end and knows that this is his last chance to get Jessup to admit that he ordered the "code red" that led to the death of a Marine under his command. The writer's intention clearly speaks to the scene being an intense confrontation between bitter adversaries. It's the climactic scene in the film, and the stakes could not be higher: if Kaffee fails, his client goes to jail for a crime he did not commit, and Jessup, the real perp, skates. So, for Kaffee, actions like, "press a lying son of a bitch for the truth," "get an egotistical prick to cut the bullshit," or "put an end to a sick game," all in some way serve the dramatic nature of the scene. If, by contrast, the actor chose to play something kindly and conciliatory like "help a buddy through a trying ordeal," they've shot way wide of the mark because that action would drain the very life out of the scene.

So, I hear you ask, what's the application here for the director?

When creating your vision for the story, again, use your common sense, serve the material, great and don't be a jerk. Don't turn the play into some kind of polemic that has nothing to do with what's on the page. There is, of course, room for radical interpretations and deconstructions of dramatic material, but even the most avant-garde versions of narrative plays – the good ones, anyway – have at their base an exploration of the core themes, even if presented in the form of a de facto critique.[2]

A striking example of a director violating the playwright's intentions concerns a production of Edward Albee's Pulitzer Prize–winning play *Who's Afraid of Virginia Woolf.* Many years ago, without Mr. Albee's permission, a professional theatre company staged the play with an all-male cast – two gay couples instead of the two heterosexual couples that Albee wrote. Mr. Albee – himself an openly gay man – was so outraged by this that he not only attempted to shut down the production but subsequently withheld the performance rights to his work for many years. "There's a certain amount of directorial creativity but it doesn't give permission to distort," he said. Not one to mince words, Mr. Albee also remarked,

> Directors seem to feel they are as creative as the playwright. Most of these changes are for commercial reasons. . . . I'm in the lucky position where I just say, "Go fuck yourself; if you don't want to do the play I wrote, do another play." The forces of darkness would back down if everybody said that.

Get the idea? Directorial creativity is great, but not to the point where it *distorts* the text. You don't want to be one of the forces of darkness, do you?

Now, on the other hand, I don't mean to suggest a cautious, timid approach to directing that would stifle a director's creativity. A production of Mr. Mamet's *Speed the Plow* took a liberty with the second scene. In the story, movie studio executive Bob Gould has a temporary secretary over to his house on the pretext that he wants to discuss a book, but in reality, he only wants to sleep with her in order to win a bet. The text calls for the scene to take place in Gould's living room, but the director set the scene outdoors, by the pool. Mr. Mamet liked the idea very much. So yes, the director took a liberty here, but one *in service of the story.*

Here's one for you to ponder. The text of Samuel Beckett's *Endgame* specifically describes the setting as "an empty room with two small windows." *That's it.* A 1986 production at the American Repertory Theatre, directed by the estimable Joanne Akalaitis, set the play in an abandoned subway replete with industrial detritus and other set pieces not specifically called for in Beckett's characteristically minimalist stage directions. The physical production, which included incidental music by Philip Glass, was meant to suggest a postapocalyptic landscape, which Ms. Akalaitis – co-founder of Mabou Mines, the venerable avant-garde theatre company – felt underscored the play's themes. Once he got wind of what Ms. Akalaitis was doing, Beckett, although he did not actually see the production, pushed back hard (or, depending on the source, lost his shit) and threatened legal action. Mr. Beckett was notoriously protective of his plays and did not tolerate what he considered to be *any* violation of the text. The production ignited a shitstorm centered around the limits of directorial liberty. So, here's the question: was that production an example of directorial overreach or a valid reimaging of the text? Do a deep dive into the production and decide for yourself.

On a very practical level, you, the director, must be aware of who you are dealing with when directing a play. Shakespeare's plays are constantly being updated and juxtaposed into different settings; sometimes the production concepts work, sometimes they don't. But Shakespeare has been dead for a very long time, so go ahead and do whatever you like, nobody is going to come after you. (Well, maybe some so-called Shakespearean scholar with some obscure bone to pick, but really, who cares? Do your thing.) Set *As You Like It* on the moon if you think it serves the material. The same holds true for anything in the public domain. But when staging plays by living playwrights, or deceased playwrights whose estates have specific production guidelines and limitations, you will, for better or worse, have to work within certain boundaries, unless you get an exemption.

A cautionary tale: in the early 1980s, the director Anne Bogart staged a student production of the Rogers and Hammerstein (R&H) musical *South Pacific* at the New York University Tisch School of the Arts. The directorial conceit was that the audience was watching a play-within-a-play performed by Navy sailors and nurses in a VA hospital as a means of dealing with various forms of posttraumatic stress disorder. Actors playing the asylum's doctors and nurses were nearly always onstage in white coats, monitoring the proceedings, taking notes on clipboards, and occasionally escorting an overwrought sailor or nurse away. I can personally attest to the fact that the production was visually arresting, extraordinarily well-acted for a student (or any other) production, and contained many of the staging and other visual trademarks that would later come to be associated with Ms. Bogart's work. She deftly shifted the focus of the play from the entrenched and insidious nature of racism to how the horrors of war impact young people, and it was riveting. *Well.* The R&H folks came to check out the production, and, to put it mildly, they flipped the fuck out. As a result, the R&H estate placed a rider in its contracts stating that any "concept" that, essentially, deviated from the original Broadway production was forbidden. Like the *Endgame* production that came a few years later, this student production also sparked an intense debate in the theatre about where directors are obligated to draw the line. (It also helped to launch Anne Bogart's directing career. Think about *that*.)

I'll leave you with this thought on the issue: in order to thrive, the theatre must be in a perpetual state of self-reinvention. It's how all great plays survive. There are countless examples of plays being reinvigorated by a fresh take by a director, whether via an overall production concept or simply how the play's core values – and, by extension, the characters – are interpreted. If theatre artists did as the R&H estate previously demanded of its canon, great plays would soon become boring, stale, repetitive, and ultimately irrelevant. (To be fair, the R&H folks gave their blessing to the recent Tony-winning Broadway revival of *Oklahoma!*, which darkly reimagined the material with, among other things, modern dress, vivid violence, heightened sexuality, color-blind casting, stripped-down musical arrangements, and a wheelchair-bound Ado Annie – the amazing Ali Stroker. So good on them – it seems they too have rolled with the times, and the results were spectacular.)

I suggest you check out the work of the great English theatre/film/opera director and author Peter Brook,[3] who sought to constantly reinvent and reinvigorate the theatre. His production concepts, although often controversial, attempted, as he put it in his classic work on theatre, *The Empty Space*, to "divide the eternal truths from the superficial variations." So have at it. Find your own way of expressing the eternal truths that you derive from the text. Just remember. . .

The story is the boss.

Working With the Writer

When staging a new play, the director will usually work closely with the playwright. Many text changes and revisions are a result of the rehearsal process; lines of dialogue or moments of action that looked or sounded good on paper just don't play well on their feet. The director can be an invaluable asset in shaping the text, and good writers will listen to their directors as well as observe for themselves what is and is not working in rehearsal. The following are a few guidelines to create an effective, professional relationship with the writer.[4]

1. *Respect the writer's work.* It's not your job to rewrite the text or skew it to how you would like to see it executed. Your job is to help writers achieve *their* vision.
2. *What to comment on*:
    a. *Scene structure.* Is the narrative line of each scene clear? Is the conflict in each scene vivid and dramatically compelling? Are there extraneous or needlessly repetitive moments?
    b. *Overall narrative.* Does the story track dramatically? Is the ending as powerful as possible Again, you're not trying to get the writer to do it your way, you're helping the story be the best it can be on its own terms.
    c. *Dialogue.* This is a tricky one because writers tend to be really protective of their dialogue. The writer's voice, first and foremost, is represented in dialogue, and a good writer works very hard to make it both sound natural and be expressive of the characters' natures, right down to the syllable. So, when reviewing dialogue, focus on brevity, clarity, and consistency to each character.
3. *Review the text in detail before beginning rehearsals.* Whatever concerns you may have should be discussed with the writer prior to the beginning of the rehearsal process. Rewrites inevitably occur during rehearsals, but the more work you can do with the writer on the text beforehand, the better.
4. *Keep your text discussions with the writer "entre nous."* It's a bad, bad, *bad* idea to discuss problems with the text in front of the

actors. It's disrespectful and can lead to free-for-alls where everyone tries to get the writer to accommodate their views. Bad juju all around. It also places writers on the spot and can make them feel the need to defend their work. You can, of course, discuss what may be problematic with the actors (up to a point; their job is to *act*, not rewrite the text) but then review any issues that come up in rehearsal with the writer *in private*.
5. *Refer to the rehearsal process.* Let the writer know what isn't working in rehearsal and *why*. But before you raise a specific issue, be sure that it's a weakness in the writing rather than a moment for which you have not found a theatrical solution.
6. *Mutual respect.* As inappropriate as it is for the director to attempt to rewrite the play, it's equally inappropriate for the writer to try to direct from the sidelines. Any notes the writer has for the actors should be communicated *in private* to the director, who will then give those adjustments to the cast. Having been a writer, director, and actor myself, I think the only thing that writers should say to the cast is "Great job!" Then they can privately kvetch their little hearts out to the director.

What's the Story?

You've read the play. A bunch of times. You're hot to direct it, and you've got tons of ideas pinballing through your head. But if you can't answer the simple question "What's the play about?", you are not ready to begin. Think about the plot-story paradigm from a layperson's point of view: someone asks you, "What's *Chinatown* about?" You reply that it's about a private detective trying to solve a really complicated murder case and, you know, there's a love story in there too. You might then get the follow-up question, "Yeah, but what's it *really* about?" Now you have to start thinking about the potent, unsettling themes that lurk in that story: power, greed, redemption, the true nature of evil, etc. In the creation of the story, writers are wont to ask themselves the same question. To address it, some form of a thematic statement is usually employed by the writer to keep the story focused on that which is essential to the hero's intentions.

This concept is by no means entirely new; it goes back as far as Aristotle. Many influential screenwriting and playwriting instructors all teach some variation of this idea. The coin of the realm in Hollywood is the *logline*: a statement that captures the genre, main characters, and essential dramatic elements of the story in one or two sentences. Michael Hauge refers to the "theme." Syd Field calls it the "interior life." From a mythological perspective, noted story analyst Christopher Vogler and the great mythologist Professor Joseph Campbell refer to the "elixir" or the "lesson learned." Michael Tierno coined the phrase "action-idea," which is derived from Aristotle's deconstruction of how stories operate. The list goes on and the nomenclatures differ, but they all essentially force the writer to answer the same question: *what is my story really about?* Let's take a brief look at the evolution of this notion for the dramatist.

A *theme*, in its most elemental form and certainly as taught in most high-school English classes, is often boiled down to a single word or two. "Redemption," "courage," "death," "love," and "good vs. evil" are all expansive, humanistic themes that great works of literature and other narrative forms explore. They might be helpful as a pedagogical jumping off point because they are easily understood, but they are fairly useless as a guide to writing a vivid and compelling piece of drama. Is there a better, more useful approach? Why yes, there is.

In his seminal text *The Art of Dramatic Writing*, Lagos Egri employs the *premise*, which is usually expressed as a philosophical aphorism:

- Don't judge a book by its cover.
- Absolute power corrupts absolutely.
- He who hesitates is lost.
- Pride goeth before the fall.
- Love conquers all.
- Trust no one.
- Appearances are often deceiving.
- Familiarity breeds contempt.
- Better to fail with honor than succeed by fraud.
- Money talks, and bullshit walks.
- Payback is a bitch.
- You can't always get what you want, but if you try, sometimes, you get what you need. (Mick Jagger and Keith Richards)
- And in the end. . . the love you take. . . is equal to the love you make. (John Lennon and Paul McCartney)

- No matter where you go, there you are. (Buckaroo Banzai)
- Don't write a check with your mouth that your ass can't cash.
- The purpose of life is a life with a purpose. So I'd rather die for a cause, than live a life that is worthless. (Immortal Technique)
- You might not have a car or big gold chain, stay true to yourself and things will change. (Snoop Dogg)
- No man's knowledge here can go beyond his experience. (John Locke)
- The life of man is solitary, poor, nasty, brutish, and short. (Thomas Hobbes, otherwise known as The Life of the Party)
- We may be through with the past, but the past isn't through with us. (*Magnolia*, Paul Thomas Anderson)

The premise helps the writer to distill and clarify the moral or philosophical underpinnings that drive the play. Notice that in these examples, even the loopy ones, there is some sense, however cryptic, of a human being who had some kind of transformative experience or, at the very least, has a specific view about life. Aphorisms both express a *theme* and often imply a *story*. A better tool with which to focus a piece of drama, no? It forces the writer to ask what the point of the story is and what the subject matter of the story is specifically meant to express. But by their nature, Egri's premises, like single-word themes, do not specifically address the cause-and-effect nature of the dramatic form. Got a better suggestion? Robert McKee does. He calls it the "Controlling Idea,"[5] and it offers a greater degree of thematic precision.

McKee writes, " A CONTROLLING IDEA may be expressed in a single sentence describing how and why life undergoes change from one condition of existence at the beginning to another at the end." Further, it "identifies the positive or negative charge of the story's critical value at the last act's climax, and it identifies the chief reason that this value has changed to its final state."[6]

The Controlling Idea takes Egri's notion of the premise and adds a *dramatic outcome* based on the success or failure of the protagonist's intention (the climax and resolution of the story) and how they change as a result. For example, McKee defines the Controlling Idea for *Dirty Harry*, the brutal, iconic thriller about a maverick cop (Clint Eastwood) tracking a serial killer as "Justice triumphs because the protagonist is more violent than the criminals."

The Controlling Idea can also express a broader conviction about life. When speaking of the outstanding film *The Reader* – a drama about a passionate love affair between a teenage boy and a woman in her thirties who had been a sadistic guard in a Nazi concentration camp – McKee suggests that the Controlling Idea is "When forgiveness is impossible, love cannot survive." A rich idea, and a story worth telling!

Let's now apply these precepts to directing.

The Unifying Principle

You, as the director, must be clear *to yourself*, in the simplest, most straightforward terms, what story you are telling and, by extension, *why* you are telling it. Again, what is your *point of view*? Let's look at a simple technique to distill and clarify your ideas: the *Unifying Principle*.

The most important thing about the Unifying Principle is that *you are passionate about it*! You are not trying to get an A on an exam; the purpose of deriving a Unifying Principle is to help you come to terms with the material. And, as we will further discuss, the Unifying Principle will keep you on track in terms of making sure that you've correctly identified the conflict in each scene so that it serves the overall story. For you, the director, the goal here is to express, in a sentence or two and in as few words as possible, what the story means *to you*.

Here's a simple template for the Unifying Principle:

> *Two forces in opposition engage in the action of the story, which leads to the resolution of the action.*

Let's break it down.

1. *Two forces in opposition.* Every story needs a conflict. If a story doesn't have a conflict, it's not a story, it's something else that would maybe like to be a story one day when it grows up. In the classic construction of a dramatic narrative, the hero/protagonist wants something. *One thing.* That goal must be clear and acute: to win the girl (or boy), to save the family farm, to get sober, to get home for the holidays, to steal the diamonds, to root out corruption in the police department, to find the Holy Grail, to survive a natural disaster, and so on.

Each story must then have forces that *oppose* the hero's desire, which can be any combination of internal, external, interpersonal, societal, and environmental. The forces of antagonism do not need to be evil or malicious; they must simply impede the hero's progress to their goal. There is a difference between an antagonist and a villain; some antagonists are actually quite well-meaning. (Parents, anyone?)
2. *The action of the story.* This is where the obstacles to the hero's goal present themselves; they form the main narrative line of the story. For a story to function, the hero, in the simplest terms, must continually *fail* to reach their goal and then keep trying to overcome the rising obstacles.
3. *The resolution of the action.* The ending of the story is really the key component in formulating the Unifying Principle. The *outcome* – that is, the protagonist's success or failure to achieve their goal and their *response* to that result – ultimately tells the audience what the story they've been watching was really about all along.

Examples of the Unifying Principle

Romeo and Juliet

Unifying Principle #1: The entrenched blind hatred of two warring factions (two forces in opposition) leads to a path of violence and death (action of the play) that leaves all their lives in ruins (resolution of the action).

Unifying Principle #2: Warring factions driven by all-consuming, blind hatred (two forces in opposition), only after having destroyed that which is most precious to them (action of the play), will finally put their differences aside (resolution of the action).

Notice the differences in the interpretation of the resolution. Number one ends the play on a purely tragic note, whereas number two offers a glimmer of hope that the Montagues and the Capulets may have finally learned to put their enmity to rest despite – or perhaps as a result of – the tragic death of the two young lovers. Two distinctly different viewpoints that will influence the emotional impact of the production.

Dirty Harry

Unifying Principle: When those in authority resort to brutality to stop depravity from flourishing, they lose their souls.

At the end of the movie, Harry kills the serial murderer known as "The Scorpio Killer" who has been taunting him throughout the story. After putting a hot one in the giggling maniac's chest that drops him into a lagoon, Harry throws his detective shield as far as he can into the water and walks away, weary and disgusted. The audience, although relieved that a wack-job killer is off the streets, is left to wonder if it was all worth it. (Obviously it was, as Harry came back for four sequels.)

Spider-Man[7]

Unifying Principle: In order for good to triumph over evil, the agents of good must be willing to embrace their calling, whatever the personal cost.

This Unifying Principle speaks to the notion that Peter Parker had a destiny that he could not deny. As his loving uncle advised him, "With great power comes great responsibility." The ending of the story particularly supports this Unifying Principle: at Norman Osborn's (Green Goblin) funeral, Peter breaks up with Mary Jane, his true love, because he knows that his secret life as Spider-Man would place her in grave danger. Mary Jane cannot understand why Peter is turning his back on her; at the same time, his best friend, Henry Osborn, has sworn an oath to kill Spider-Man to avenge the death of his father. Peter not only gives up the woman he loves but he places himself on a deadly collision course with his best friend, who does not know he is actually Spider-Man. The choice to embrace becoming Spider-Man costs Peter Parker everything.

The Band's Visit

Unifying Principle: People from disparate cultures that do not understand or trust each other are united by the universal human experiences of longing, regret, and hope.

Both the film and Broadway musical versions of *The Band's Visit* concern an Egyptian military band – in Israel to play a gig – that gets stranded overnight in a small, remote Israeli village. Initially wary of each other, by the next morning both the Israeli and the Egyptian characters have deeply bonded by sharing life's simple but essential pleasures: food, music, love, and family.

Henry V: Two Film Versions

Lord Laurence Olivier and Sir Kenneth Branagh each directed and starred in film adaptations of Shakespeare's *Henry V*, some 45 years apart. Both films were groundbreaking, but because they were distinct products of their times, they could not have been more different in their approaches to the material.

Olivier's version was an innovative and rousing film, a valentine to English manhood, and a colorful, entertaining exhortation to, in the words of Winston Churchill, "Never give in, never give in, never; never; never; never – in nothing, great or small, large or petty – never give in except to convictions of honor and good sense." Released in 1944, the film was conceived top to bottom to uplift the war-weary British audience's flagging spirits, from Olivier's charming, theatrical, but (in retrospect) hammy performance, to the colorful pageantry and storybook sets, to the portrayal of the seemingly effortless victory the badly outnumbered English garnered against the French armies. Olivier's Henry happily emerged from the climactic battle without so much as a scratch or a hair out of place on his perfectly coiffed head. Even his horse looked spiffy.

> *Olivier's Unifying Principle: Even against overwhelming odds, the indomitable spirit of a great leader will inspire his charges to the pinnacle of victory.*

Branagh, a product of the post–Vietnam War generation, took not only a sober, more realistic view of the horrors of war but also created a complex, vulnerable hero who, despite his keen intellect, undeniable courage, and canny sense of leadership is fraught with self-doubt, rage, and a burning desire to prove himself in the eyes of his countrymen and the world. It is, in essence, a coming-of-age story. Released in 1989, the film's overall palette is dark and roughhewn, the colors subdued, and the interior spaces often small and cramped, all lending the film a sense of gritty realism. At the end of Branagh's version, Henry, battle-fatigued and grim, walks across the smoldering, corpse-strewn battlefield, his hard-won victory bringing him no joy; the cost of war is just too great to warrant celebration. We see, finally, that the boy-king has grown into full manhood and a wise, powerful leader.

> *Branagh's Unifying Principle: To become a great leader, one must prevail over the most extreme tests of wisdom and courage.*

Please note that one Unifying Principle does not completely cancel out or deny the other. Both films contain moments that, so to speak, cross over. But the *primary focus* in each interpretation of the story is vastly different.

Real-Life Examples

After you have solidified your Unifying Principle, take a moment to think of nonfictional examples. You want to make sure that the thematic principles you are going to portray are true to life and not just expedient to stage a piece of drama. What people or actual events speak to your Unifying Principle? Stay away from other fictional examples – look to how your idea resonates to real life.

> *Romeo and Juliet*: The Hatfields and McCoys. During the Civil War, the Confederate Hatfields took issue with the Union-supporting McCoys. Murder, kidnapping, and other horrific acts of violence went on for years, leaving both families in ruins for generations.
> *The Band's Visit*: African American activist Darryl Davis met with hundreds of white supremacists and KKK members. Through his interactions with them, over 200 people renounced their affiliation with the Klan. Mr. Davis was able to show the former racists that both black and white people share the same humanity.

Nonnarrative and Nonlinear Forms

Many narrative works have minimal or no plot structure, or they are held together by a common theme, rather than an explicit arch storyline with a single protagonist. Even in these cases, the need for a Unifying Principle is still absolutely essential for the director.

For example, Ntozake Shange's revolutionary theatre piece *For Colored Girls Who Have Considered Suicide/When the Rainbow Is Enuf* is a series of poetic monologues, accompanied by music and dance, all of which deal with various forms of sexism, racism, and exploitation experienced by African American women. Produced on Broadway in the mid-1970s, *For Colored Girls* is a beautifully written, heartfelt piece of theatre that deals with many volatile sociopolitical issues that have, sadly, yet to find satisfactory resolution in our society.

In formulating a Unifying Principle, one might argue that the common antagonist is a *society* that devalues and debases women. From my point of view, even though Ms. Shange dramatizes numerous situations – including abandonment, rape, and domestic violence – that are painful, confusing, and sometimes downright horrifying, there is an underpinning of hope throughout the piece. So, a Unifying Principle might be, "*Those who have been marginalized by society will overcome oppression and self-actualize through the power of love, sisterhood, and unity.*" This Unifying Principle will help the director identify the forces of oppression and highlight how the characters overcome them.

Conclusion

Feel free to make this formula work for you. Tweak it however you want to. Make up your own. What you need, finally, is a simple statement that is based on *cause* and *effect*, paying particular mind to how you wish to portray the *outcome* of the story. The Unifying Principle, or whatever variation you might find useful, exists to help you clarify your point of view on the material and make sure every element, including your instructions to the actors, contributes to the clear execution of your vision of the story.

Exercises

1. Come up with a Unifying Principle for three of the films or plays in this chapter.
2. Come up with two different Unifying Principles for three films or plays of your choice.
3. Add a real-life example to each of your Unifying Principles.

Notes

1. Some writers claim that they never consciously consider the thematic implications of their stories when writing them. Fair enough, but those themes are still in evidence and should still be examined accordingly.
2. For more on this approach to theatre, check out the Mabou Mines theatre company. They have been doing experimental and reimagined adaptations of classic plays for 50 years.
3. For starters, check out Mr. Brook's Royal Shakespeare Company (RSC) productions of *A Midsummer Night's Dream*; *Marat/Sade*; the epic *Mahabarata*; and his deconstruction of Bizet's opera *Carmen*.
4. For information on the contractual issues governing writer-director collaboration in feature films and television, visit the Writers Guild of America (WGA) website.
5. For more detailed information on the mechanics of generating the Controlling Idea and its full utility for the writer, read *Story*, McKee's comprehensive book on the art of screenwriting. Many of the principles in *Story* are applicable to playwriting and other narrative forms.
6. *Story* by Robert McKee, page 115.
7. 2002 version, directed by Sam Raimi, starring Tobey Maguire, Kirsten Dunst, and James Franco.

Works Cited

The Adventures of Buckaroo Banzai Across the 8th Dimension. Directed by W. D. Richter. 20th Century Fox, 1984.
American Graffiti. Directed by George Lucas. A Lucasfilm Ltd/Coppola Co. Production, 1973.
The Band's Visit. Directed by Eran Kolirin. Sony Pictures, 2007.
Beckett, Samuel. *Endgame*. New York, Grove Press, 1957.
Brook, Peter. *The Empty Space*. London, Penguin Books, 2008.
Bruder, Melissa, Lee Michael Cohn, et al. *A Practical Handbook for the Actor*. New York, Vintage Books, 1986.
Chinatown. Directed by Roman Polanski. Paramount Pictures, 1974.
Dirty Harry. Directed by Don Siegel. Warner Bros., 1971.
Egri, Lajos. *The Art of Dramatic Writing: Its Basis in the Creative Interpretation of Human Motives, Etc*. London, Sir Isaac Pitman & Sons, 1950.
Get Out. Director/screenwriter Jordan Peele. Universal Pictures, 2017.
The Godfather. Director/co-screenwriter Francis Ford Coppola. Paramount Pictures, 1972.
The Godfather Part II. Director/co-screenwriter Francis Ford Coppola. Paramount Pictures, 1974.
Henry V. Directed by Kenneth Branagh. The Samuel Goldwyn Company, 1989.
Henry V. Directed by Laurence Olivier. United Artists, 1944.
Immortal Technique. "The Martyr." *The Martyr*, 2011.
Jagger, Mick, and Keith Richards. "You Can't Always Get What You Want." *Let It Bleed*, 1969.
Lawrence of Arabia. Directed by David Lean. Columbia Pictures, 1962.
Lennon, John, and Paul McCartney. "The End." *Abbey Road*, 1969.
Mamet, David. *Speed-the-Plow*. New York, Grove Press, 1988.
McKee, Robert. *Story: Substance, Structure, Style and the Principles of Screenwriting*. New York, Regan Books, 1997.
Miller, Arthur. *Death of a Salesman*. New York, Dramatists Play Service, 1980.
Munich. Directed by Steven Spielberg. Universal Pictures, 2005.

Parasite. Director/screenwriter Bong Joon Ho and Jin-won Han. Neon, 2019.
The Reader. Directed by Stephen Daldry. The Weinstein Company, 2008.
Rocky. Directed by John Avildsen. United Artists, 1976.
Rodgers, Richard, et al. *South Pacific: A Musical Play*. New York, Random House, 1949.
The Searchers. Directed by John Ford. Warner Bros., 1956.
Shakespeare, William. "The Merchant of Venice." In *Riverside Shakespeare*. Boston, Houghton Mifflin Company, 1973.
Shakespeare, William. "Romeo and Juliet." In *Riverside Shakespeare*. Boston, Houghton Mifflin Company, 1973.
Shange, Ntozake. *For Colored Girls Who Have Considered Suicide/When the Rainbow Is Enuf*. New York, Macmillan Publishing Company, 1977.
Snoop Dogg. "Be Thankful." *Best by Far*, 2000.
South Park. Created by Matt Stone and Trey Parker. Comedy Central, 1997. Television.
Spider-Man. Directed by Sam Raimi. Columbia Pictures, 2002.
Williams, Tennessee. *A Streetcar Named Desire*. New York, New American Library, 1947.
Wilson, August. *Fences*. New York, Samuel French, 1986.
The Wizard of Oz. Directed by Victor Fleming. MGM, 1939.

3
ACTIONS

Webster's dictionary defines an action as "the physical pursuance of a specific goal." This is where the rubber hits the road in terms of good acting technique, because the only thing an actor can effectively play is an *action*. Actors cannot play an emotional or psychological state of being without resorting to *indicating*, which, once again, means showing the audience what the actor thinks the character should be thinking or feeling in an inauthentic fashion. In layperson's terms, indicating means *faking it*. (Of course, as the great comedian George Burns once remarked, "The key to success is sincerity. If you can fake that, you've got it made.") The audience *always* knows when an actor is full of shit, even if they can't articulate why they feel that way. Truthful behavior that fulfills the needs of the story is, in theory, the endgame of any acting technique, although some are absolutely more effective than others. (That's another discussion, over beer number two.) So, as per one of the core tenets of this book, a director must understand the difference between a playable and nonplayable acting choice, so let's look at physical actions, which form the cornerstone of not only good acting choices but also the director's framework with which to break down a script.

The Mechanics of Physical Action

In his *Method of Physical Acting*, Stanislavski (you know, the Russian guy who founded the Moscow Art Theatre and helped invent modern acting and stuff) said that an action should accomplish three main purposes for the actor: 1. help tell the story; 2. connect the actor to the other actors on stage; and 3. inspire the actor's imagination and creativity. Everything we will discuss in terms of how actions operate will fulfill one of those three essential criteria.

Think of an action as a declaration of purpose. It tells the actor what they want to accomplish in the scene. A playable action has a very simple construction: *an active verb + a clearly defined goal* that can be stated in one simple phrase. "To push" is not a complete action; "to push a coward to take a stand" is a complete, playable action. "To prevent" is not a complete action. What are you preventing? Who are you talking to? "To prevent a friend from making a terrible mistake" is a complete action. Actions should use as few words as possible to get the point across. If an action is overly long and complicated, the actor will lose focus due to a lack of clarity and specificity.

Even though actions are performed under imaginary circumstances, they are *common tasks* – things we all understand and have probably done at some point in our lives. Even if the actor hasn't actually performed a particular action in their own life, that's okay; as long as they can *imagine* it, they can do it.

Here are the guidelines that make up a playable action, which we will then apply in Chapter 4 to analyze a scene.

1. *An action must be physically capable of being accomplished.* An action must, first and foremost, be something the actor can actually *do*. The litmus test is simple: can the actor turn to the person next to them and do it *right now*? The task should be accomplishable in *real time* in the playing of the scene. The actor can "ask for a big favor" or "make a sincere apology" immediately. They cannot act "flow into an alternate state of consciousness by drinking in a cup of cosmic knowledge." Again, an ACTIVE VERB + a CLEARLY DEFINED GOAL.
2. *An action has its test in the other person.* Remember, the actor plays an action in real time, interacting moment to moment with the other person(s) in the scene. So, at any moment, actors should be able to identify – *via the other actor's behavior, not the script* – the

degree to which they are succeeding or failing to accomplish their goals. For instance, if an actor is playing "to win a potential ally's support," at any moment they should be able to gauge whether or not their acting partner is behaving supportively. This is very important because it encourages the actor stay connected to the *truth of the moment*. As a director, one of the most helpful things you can do for actors, especially when they are struggling, is to direct them to respond to what is really going on in the here and now. Get them out of their heads and into the moment!

3. *An action has a clearly definable cap.* The cap is the manifestation of the goal that is defined in the action. Although the text ultimately will dictate the success or failure of an action in a given scene, the cap must materialize *in the other person's behavior* as well as in the text. For you poker players out there, you're looking for the *tell*. What will tell the actor that the other person is doing what they want? A gesture? A facial expression? Tears? Laughter? A tone of voice? An emotional response? It could be any or all of these things, in any combination. If, for instance, the actor is playing "to demand an apology," they are looking for a clear sign(s) in the other person that unequivocally evinces an apology. Again, *behavior*, not dialogue. So, using common sense, if the other actor has a line that says, "Fine, yes, I apologize," but that line is delivered with bitterness and anger, well, clearly, the cap of that action has not been achieved.

4. *An action does not presuppose an emotional state.* An action should never be based on the actor having to feel anything in particular, nor should it be predicated on the other person in the scene having to be in a specific state of emotion. The reasons for this are twofold: first, any acting choice predicated on an emotion will make the actor self-conscious. An actor's attention should be, with few exceptions, outwardly directed. A choice based on an emotion, like "to show someone how angry I am," will force the actor to generate and maintain an emotional state in the scene, and thus they will be unable to respond freely and spontaneously to the other actor moment-to-moment. Unless you're one of those freak-brain, one

in a million, simultaneous multitaskers, human beings can only have their attention in one place at a time; when actors have their attention on *themselves*, they are not acting in the moment.

Second, to reduce a scene to a single emotional state is both untrue to human nature and limiting for the actor. In his first autobiography, *Rewrites: A Memoir*, the great Neil Simon related a story about having a knock-down, drag-out screamer of a fight with his wife, Joan. He describes a moment when the two of them, in the middle of the argument, stopped fighting and started laughing, suddenly aware of how ridiculously they were both behaving. And then, a few minutes later, the cups and saucers were flying once again. This is life, in all its glorious contradictions. So, if the actor has conceptualized the scene as predicated on a single, usually obvious and cliché emotion (a funeral is sad, a wedding is happy, etc.), the myriad other possibilities that a strong action, the text, the actor's own impulses, and the truthful moment-to-moment reality that the scene might offer are completely negated in favor of a pre-planned and pedestrian result.

Finally, to presuppose an emotional state in your acting partner is another dirt road to nowhere. "To get a friend to stop being mad at me" will leave the actor high and dry if the other player in the scene is not angry. And here's what tends to happen: the actor playing that action will pretend the other person *is* angry, which leads to an untruthful performance. And as previously discussed, the audience *always* detects an actor's disconnect from the truth of the moment. The need to perform an action presupposes not a predetermined set of emotions but the need to somehow bring order to a chaotic situation; if the conflict in the scene has been correctly identified, then the chosen action should work regardless of how the other actor is initially behaving in the scene.

5. *An action is not an errand.* An errand is an action that requires no response from the other person in the scene. All the actor needs to do is say the words, and the errand is accomplished. Every action should have a level of *accountability*: is the actor working moment to moment to achieve their action as per numbers three and four? Is the other person responding positively? Also,

an errand indicates that the actor has not really examined the text carefully. "To say hello" is an errand; "to welcome friends to a celebration" is not an errand because it demands that the actor make sure the other players in the scene feel welcome. (The next chapter will deconstruct this dynamic in great detail.)

6. *An action is nonmanipulative.* The core of this tenet is essential to understand a character's mindset and to ensure that actors will fully commit to their choices.

Every scene is a *problem* that each character is attempting to solve in service of their overall goal. The dramatist has created a world that is somehow chaotic and out of balance, so *every action must be designed to create order from the character's point of view.* An action may indeed create conflict when juxtaposed against the other actors' intentions in a scene, but its *intent* is *to fix the problem*, even if the audience finds it wrongheaded, misguided, or self-destructive. People always do what they think best at a particular moment in time, even if later on they regret or rethink their choices and change course. But in order for actors to fully commit to what they are doing, they have to come from the position that they are *right*. Even the most seemingly negative or destructive character believes, in any given situation, that they are acting *correctly*. This dictum is most clearly understood when figuring out how to play a villain or a character of questionable moral fiber.

The titular character in the television thriller *Dexter* (brilliantly played by Michael C. Hall) tortures and kills criminals and various other wrongdoers. What he does to his victims is horrific, but Dexter believes he is serving a higher good by ridding the world of evil. The ends, for him, easily justify the means. He also derives, at times, nearly orgasmic pleasure from the killings. So, when the actor plays Dexter in a torture scene, any action that paints him as evil would be manipulative. It would make him "wrong." "To torture for pleasure" does not speak to the inner moral imperative that directs Dexter's behavior. A better, nonmanipulative action for Dexter in such a scene would be "to teach a harsh lesson," "to force a sinner to repent," or "to get a transgressor to accept their fate." These actions illuminate Dexter's state of mind to the audience: he sees himself as an avenging angel whose mission is to cleanse the world of malignant wrong-doers. Dexter is attempting to bring order to the chaos of the world that he inhabits. He is, from his point of view, acting *correctly*.

The other aspect of a manipulative action is that it centers on getting the other person to feel something rather than to *do* something. Attempting to manipulate another person's emotions is kind of a jerk move to begin with, and it also does not give the actor a clear understanding of the scene or, by extension, a clear cap. "To make someone angry" or "to make someone feel sadness" is not a good action. To what end is the actor seeking to evoke those emotions in the other person? What satisfaction might the character derive? Answer those questions, and the actor will find a better action because they will have a deeper understanding of the character's need. Emotional displays might be indicative of an action's success or failure at any particular moment in the scene, but they are not an end in themselves.

7. *An action should be fun to do.* As per Stanislavski, one of the criteria for a good action is that it inspires the actor. Actors should be excited to play the scene; if they feel like the action is dull and uninspiring or merely obligatory, that attitude will affect the performance. The best actions are the ones that bring actors to life and inspire a sense of play. So, a good action can be, variously, challenging, intense, cool, silly, frustrating, or anything else that evokes a visceral response and makes the actor want to leap in and act the scene. Being totally engaged in acting the scene is *fun*, even when actors are crying their eyes out.

Semantics is helpful in choosing a fun action. Actions should not feel dry or academic; actors and directors should utilize language that is familiar, real, and vernacular. Actions can be rough, impolite, or even politically incorrect. Don't sugarcoat! Actions have to feel real and accessible; they help actors be honest about what the scene really means to them. So, a more fun version of a bland, vanilla, wordy action like "get someone to do what they previously agreed to do" might be something like, "hold a snake to their word," "enforce an iron-clad contract," or "get a shady partner to stop fucking with me."

See the difference?

The use of semantics, just like language itself, is highly malleable. People use words differently, and indeed the meaning and emotional impact of certain words or phrases are often a product of a person's environment, upbringing, and education. A Southern phrase that I love is "Bless his heart." To a non-Southerner, it sounds like a sweet little benediction, but in local parlance it means, "He's not very bright. Go easy on him."

A colleague of mine encourages his students to come up with actions that are really colorful, personal, and colloquial, such as "let a douche know I got the 411 on his ass" and "make a fool eat his heart out." For Lady Macbeth, in the "Screw your courage to the sticking place" speech,[1] the student actor came up with "to man up a milquetoast little bitch." So, the director can help the actors by suggesting actions that they can directly relate to as human beings.

8. *An action is specific.* As Stanislavski said, "Generality is the enemy of art." Specificity in choosing actions works on two levels: first, it should express a clear point of view in the scene (this will be better understood in Chapter 4). Second, an action should not be vague and "all-purpose." Actions like "to get what I want," "to get what I need," and "to get someone to give me something" are so vague they could ostensibly be plugged into any scene; thus, they are essentially meaningless. For the actor, a vague, nonspecific action does not help create a strong point of view from which to play the scene. As per the example in number 7, "get someone to do what they previously agreed to do" is not nearly as specific as "hold a snake to their word."

9. *An action should fulfill the intentions of the dramatist.* We've already discussed this at length, but once again – who's the boss? That's right, the story. So, every choice an actor makes must serve the story, and ultimately it is the director's responsibility to make sure that happens.

Defining Labels in Actions

Take notice of the fact that many actions contain a descriptive noun: friend, sinner, etc. The use of descriptive nouns is an extremely efficient way to pinpoint one character's emotional relationship to another. I refer to them as *defining labels*. Why do we use them? Because a character's point of view toward the other person in a given scene does not necessarily align with the relationship indicated in the text. Indeed, the relationship between two people can, and usually does in a well-written story, change profoundly as the story progresses.

Let's take the idea of a marriage. Contained within that formal designation are many nuanced interactions that constantly change and redefine the nature of the relationship. For instance, married partners might be, variously, lovers, friends, allies, business associates, adversaries, etc. Additionally, one partner might view the other in a completely different light at the same moment; a scene between a married couple might, in essence, be an encounter between a student and teacher, an accuser and the accused, a caretaker and a dependent, etc. Stories that explicate the dissolution of a marriage[2] can be tracked by how each person views the other in each scene. Throughout the entire story, the characters are a married couple; that imaginary circumstance is fixed, but it does not provide the actor with any insight that can be acted upon. So, the good director has an understanding of the ever-shifting relationship and plots that progression out scene by scene.

A defining label, because it creates a strong and specific point of view, will also affect the actor's behavior in a scene. It's like a filtered lens that colors how one person perceives the other person's behavior. An actor will approach playing "to wise up a lost friend" differently than "to wise up a smart-ass." Wouldn't you talk to a friend differently than you would to a smart-ass, even if trying to accomplish the same goal? And just to get really meta here, in the script the relationship might literally be a friendship, but in a given scene, one friend might regard the other as a smart-ass. (All of my friends regard me as a smart-ass, and vice versa. Hey, it works for us.)

The point here is, define the relationship scene by scene!

There are many actions that do not include a defining label. Sometimes they are not necessary, either because the relationship is of secondary or no importance or the relationship is so self-evident that it doesn't need further clarification. If you are an actor playing a detective who is interrogating a suspect whom your character knows is lying, "put an end to a pointless charade" might be all that you need; "get a *liar* to end a pointless charade" is just redundant in this instance. That said, the point here is, if you need to assign a defining label to an action, be sure it specifically expresses the character's point of view *in the scene*. Finally, in the name of clarity, avoid the use of "someone" because it always dilutes the specificity of the action.

"Prevent someone from making a critical mistake" is far less playable and dynamic than "prevent a babe in the woods from making a critical mistake."

Conclusion

An understanding of the mechanics of a playable acting choice is essential for both actors and directors. Strong, clear, stage-worthy actions form the foundation of a solid dramatic framework for every scene in the play. In the next chapter, we will look at the Practical Aesthetics approach to script analysis, which will help the director create that framework.

A Brief and Very Incomplete List of Playable Actions in No Particular Order

Note #1: It's generally better to find a more specific verb than "get," because every action is about getting something. In the list below, I've left "get" in several of the actions. See if you can come up with a better verb. If you feel "get" serves the purpose of the scene, then let it fly.

Note #2: In many of these examples, the defining label is intentionally left blank and is indicated by[. . .]. It's important to note that any defining label in any action can be changed to suit the needs of a given scene.

Note #3: If you need to gender a defining label, do it on the basis of the gender of the other character in the scene.

- To win a skeptic's trust
- To enforce an iron-clad contract
- To hold a slimeball to his word
- To help a friend over a rough patch
- To end a sick game
- To correct a terrible false impression
- To renegotiate a bad deal
- To force a fuckup to see that it's game over
- To win an ally
- To get [. . .] on my team
- To lay down the law
- To draw the dividing line
- To encourage [. . .] to take a big step [or big risk]
- To retrieve what's rightfully mine

- To call in a debt
- To confront a bully to stand down
- To get [. . .] to see the big picture
- To convince a dreamer to give up a delusion
- To dive to the bottom of a mystery
- To get a shady partner to stop fucking with me
- To uncover a lie
- To expose a fraud
- To close the deal
- To get [. . .] to throw me a lifeline
- To inspire an act of courage [or sacrifice]
- To implore a loved one to take care of me
- To get a friend to share a burden
- To persuade a superior to make an exception
- To get [. . .] to look the other way
- To boost a[. . .]'s self-confidence
- To help a friend see the bright side
- To push a child to stand on their own
- To force [. . .] to face their problems
- To force a slacker to take responsibility
- To inspire [. . .] to share my dream
- To get a bro to give me a break
- To teach [. . .] to see the errors of their ways
- To get [. . .] to respect my beliefs
- To seek a potential ally's support
- To get a man-baby to grow up
- To disprove a vicious lie [or false allegation]
- To get [. . .] to respect my boundaries
- To get a loved one to let me go
- To rouse a shrinking violet to take a stand
- To get [. . .] to admit their guilt
- To get a jerk off my back
- To demand an apology
- To spur a coward to grow a pair
- To dare a screwup to believe they can do better
- To make amends for a big mistake
- To get a wuss to man up

- To draw a wallflower out of their shell
- To explain [or clarify] a difficult decision
- To teach a newbie the ropes
- To kick an asshole to the curb
- To hold a snake to their word
- To get a superior to see the real offense
- To get a well-deserved pass
- To burn down a fatuous argument
- To warn a rival they're headed for a big fall
- To help a friend see how good they've got it
- To negotiate the deal of a lifetime
- To get an expert to greenlight a big decision
- To demand a partner pull their weight
- To sever a bogus contract
- To negotiate a better deal

Defining Labels

Positive/Sympathetic

- Friend
- Ally
- Loved one
- Bro
- Buddy
- Partner
- Mentor
- Pal
- Lover
- Caretaker
- Teacher
- Lost soul
- Babe in the woods
- Wiz
- Soulmate

Negative/Adversarial

- Asshole
- Jerk

- Weasel
- Slimeball
- Punk
- Slacker
- Enemy
- Numb-nuts
- Fucktard
- Snake
- Sinner
- Wuss
- Pussy
- Scaredy-cat
- Con artist
- Creep
- Liar
- Man-baby
- Clueless dipshit
- Snowflake
- Energy vampire
- Spoiled brat
- Bitch
- Accuser
- Wiseass
- Egomaniac
- Shrinking violet
- Competitor
- Hover-parent
- Phony
- Pompous ass

Neutral (Can Go Either Way)
- Associate
- Newbie
- Student
- Neophyte
- Dependent
- Dreamer

- Authority figure
- Boss

Exercises

These exercises will help you to practice creating a conflict by making sure that the chosen actions work in opposition. If you can get a couple of actors (or friends with nothing better to do) to read the scenes out loud, that would be helpful and fun.

1. Neutral Scenes

Assign different sets of actions to the dialogue. Try the same actions with different defining labels. Make sure there is a conflict!

Neutral Scene 1

A: Did everything work out?
B: Yeah. Thanks.
A: Need anything?
B: No, you've done enough.
A: You sure?
B: Yeah. I'm good.
A: Alright. Take care.
B: Thanks. You too.

Neutral Scene 2

For this scene, before assigning actions, add the following imaginary circumstances:

- A relationship
- A place
- A prior circumstance leading up to this conversation

A: I had no idea this would be so much fun!
B: You didn't.
A: No, I really didn't.
B: I'm surprised.
A: Why?

B: Because I thought you were different.
A: What do you mean?
B: Just more in touch with what's really going on.
A: You're taking all the fun out, now.
B: How so?
A: Forget it.

2. Breakup Scene

As per the neutral scenes, assign different actions and defining labels in different combinations, once again making sure the opposing actions always create a conflict. Then add given circumstances, a place, etc. Remember that a "breakup" is not limited to a romantic relationship.

A: Things are not working out.
B: I know.
A: I wish they were different.
B: Yeah, me too.
A: We need to take a break from each other.
B: You think that'll solve our problems?
A: I don't know. But it's what's best right now.
B: If that's what you want, fine.
A: I wish things were different.
B: Do you?
A: I just said that I did.

Notes

1 *Macbeth*, Act I, Scene 7.
2 A few excellent films on this subject: Ingmar Bergman's *Scenes From a Marriage* (Liv Ullman); Noah Baumbach's *Marriage Story* (Adam Driver, Scarlett Johansson); Sam Mendes' *Revolutionary Road* (Michelle Williams, Leonardo DiCaprio); Michelangelo Antonioni's *La Notte* (Marcello Mastroianni, Jeanne Moreau).

Works Cited

Dexter. Created by James Manos, Jr. Showtime Networks, 2006. Television.
Shakespeare, William. "Macbeth." In *Riverside Shakespeare*. Boston, Houghton Mifflin Company, 1973.
Simon, Neil. *Rewrites: A Memoir*. New York, Touchstone, 1998.
Toporkov, Vasiliĭ Osipovich. *Stanislavski in Rehearsal: The Final Years*. New York, Routledge/Theatre Arts Book, 1998.

4
PRACTICAL AESTHETICS SCRIPT ANALYSIS

A (Very) Brief Overview of Practical Aesthetics

The Practical Aesthetics acting technique was originally conceived by David Mamet and then taught by him to a group of NYU students (including your humble author), who eventually went on to form the Atlantic Theater Company. Since those initial workshops in the early 1980s, thousands of students have trained in Practical Aesthetics at numerous institutions and in private workshops, including my own. It is now considered a major American acting technique, along with the Method, the Adler technique, the Meisner technique, etc. Practical Aesthetics was popularized by the publication of *A Practical Handbook for the Actor*, which has, to date, sold over 330,000 copies and is the single best-selling acting book ever written. At the time of its publication, it created something of a stir in the theatrical world: many actors, directors (Sidney Lumet and Robert Benton among them), and other creative practitioners hailed it as both revelatory and revolutionary, while others took great umbrage at the technique in both theory and practice and branded the young authors as heretics and goofballs. We pissed off a lot of people – it was really fun.

The technique is based on the later works of Stanislavski, which stressed the importance of playing specific "psychophysical" actions on stage in his Method of Physical Action. Practical Aesthetics also incorporates Stoic philosophy, the work of child psychologist Bruno Bettelheim (whose book on fairy tales, *The Uses of Enchantment*, profoundly explicates how an audience imaginatively engages in a story), the core principles of Aristotle, and several others.

The Practical Aesthetics philosophy of acting can be distilled down into two major components: *action* and *moment*. The process of delving deeply into a character's true need in every scene, and then finding a playable *action* to express that understanding, is the most essential component of the actor's (and director's) preparation. *Moment* denotes the ability of the actor to play a scene spontaneously and freely moment to moment based on their chosen action, without preconception. An understanding of the relationship between words and actions is of paramount importance in Practical Aesthetics. The great director Peter Brook put it like this:

> A word does not start as a word – it is an end product which begins as an impulse, stimulated by attitude and behavior which dictate the need for expression. This process occurs inside the dramatist; it is repeated inside the actor. Both may only be conscious of the words, but both for the author and then for the actor the word is a small visible portion of a gigantic unseen formation. Some writers attempt to nail down their meaning and intentions in stage directions and explanations, yet we cannot help being struck by the fact that the best dramatists explain themselves the least. They recognize that the only way to find the true path to the speaking of a word is through a process that parallels the original creative one. This can neither be bypassed nor simplified.

Thus, actors and directors must begin with an understanding of the words – the dialogue – within the *context* of the imaginary circumstances of the scene. We used to say that actors *prepare so they can improvise*. Of course, the actor must adhere to the script, staging, director's instructions, etc., but within those confines, an essential element of the actor's craft is the ability to respond impulsively and truthfully to their scene partners in pursuit of their action. In the parlance of the trade, the good actor is always "in the moment." It's more like a Grateful Dead jam (on a good night) than a rigid, note-for-note classical music concert. Another way to frame Practical Aesthetics is that actors must *think before they act* (preparation), so they can *act before they think* (performing the scene). Truthful behavior from an actor is always a result of playing the scene *as it is actually unfolding*, rather than based on any preplanned ideas. This is a trope of good acting that extends beyond Practical Aesthetics.

What follows is an overview of the Practical Aesthetics approach to script analysis. This process will help the director gain a deep understanding of every character's intention in every scene.

The Scene

A classically constructed dramatic narrative is broken up into a series of *scenes* wherein a protagonist attempts to overcome the mounting obstacles to their ultimate goal. The progression of a narrative works on a cause-and-effect basis: protagonists will generally *fail* in their attempts to accomplish their actions in a given scene, and based on what they learn or discover, they then decide to take *another* action in pursuit of their overall desire and off we go to the next scene in the story. Even the occasional success will lead the character to, accordingly, take the next step. So, the correct unit for the actor's focus is not the overarching intention in the entire narrative, but the *scene*. The actor parses a script one scene at a time, one *action* at a time. This is also, not surprisingly, how an audience processes a story. Likewise, the director will analyze and then rehearse a play *one scene at a time*.

The most single most important element of the director's preparation is to delineate the dramatic conflict in each scene.

In order to ensure that the story is told clearly and vividly, it is the director's responsibility to make sure that the actors' choices polarize the conflict to the greatest degree possible in each scene. The characters' needs must play in opposition to each other, or the scene will not function dramatically. Now, a lot of this falls on the writer; unfortunately, especially in television, many scenes are purely expositional and there is little or no conflict. You know what I'm talking about: those interminable, God-awful, boring scenes in procedural dramas where some tech-savvy Gen Z or Millennial character – what luck! – finds that essential piece of info on the Internet, and then the other characters talk about it while the audience either grits their teeth and hopes for the story to get going again or they fall asleep (re the latter: guilty as charged). Remember, the audience doesn't want information, they want *drama*. Hey, what can I tell ya? Sometimes the writing sucks. Do your best and call it a day.

Just as the mechanics of a plot do not tell us what a piece of drama is really about, the same holds true for the actor when analyzing a scene. What is *literally* happening in a scene does not necessarily articulate what that experience means to the character internally. Let's revisit the idea of the breakup of a romantic relationship. There are undoubtedly hundreds (thousands? millions?) of scenes in which one person is breaking up with another. But to tell the actor to simply play "break up with him" is not a specific acting choice because it does not reveal the *nature* of the scene. The actor needs to play an action that will illuminate the character's *point of view* to the audience.

Michelle is breaking up with Bob. In version A, Michelle is very much in love with Bob but has decided that the relationship will not work out. It's not easy for Michelle, because she knows that Bob will be devastated, and she cares about him. So, the actor playing Michelle might choose to play an action like "to let a loved one down easy" or "to clarify a difficult decision."

In version B, Michelle is fed up with Bob's abusive behavior. (You can fill in the blank here – drugs, womanizing, crime, bad sex, incessant flatulence – whatever it took to get Michelle to the point where she thinks Bob is a total asshole.) In this scenario, Michelle has had enough and wants it over, once and for all, right now. So, the actor playing Michelle might choose an action like "get a dickhead to hit the bricks" or "put a loser in his place."

In both versions, the plot is the same: Michelle is ending the relationship. But we can see that the points of view and attendant emotional temperaments of the two scenes could not be more different. The chosen actions, by necessity, must both express the characters' points of view and be *playable* by the actors. This begins with coming to an understanding of the relationship between the *words* and the *intention*, which may or may not directly express the characters' desires. People often speak to their intentions indirectly for myriad reasons; "Have a nice day" can mean anything from "I wish you well" to "Thanks for your help" to "Go fuck yourself." It is the job of the actor and, by extension, the director, to come to an understanding of what the words mean *within the context of the scene*.

The next section will employ these principles in formal text analysis. We'll start with single scenes, and then in Chapter 5 we will apply these principles to the overall analysis of a character.

Scene Analysis: A Three-Step Process

The point of scene analysis is to help the actor find a strong, simple, playable action that gets under the character's skin. It is also extremely useful for directors because it will help them create a road map for the entire story and bring to life the dramatic conflict in every scene.

It's important for the director to remember that each character in a scene must be analyzed *separately*. The overall shape and structure of the scene will eventually be based on the juxtaposition of the two characters' actions, but each character's analysis will inevitably be different.

STEP ONE: *What Is the Character* Literally *Doing?*

The purpose of the first step is to understand what is on the page without rushing to judgment or interpretation before taking the time to investigate the inner values of the scene, which we will do in Step Two. So, the analytical process begins with an objective look at the character.

The answer to the question "What is the character literally doing?" is a simple declarative sentence that adheres to the following:

1. *Is noninterpretive.* In this step it is important to refrain from making any judgments of the character's mental or emotional state. Usually, those snap judgments are based on a cursory reading of the lines and lock in a perfunctory, obvious interpretation of the scene. Again, what characters say may have nothing to do with their true intentions.
2. *Speaks only to the FACTS of the scene.* Don't make stuff up that isn't there! Period!
3. *Does not factor in other scenes in the story, either before or after the scene being analyzed.* Do not go outside the boundaries of the scene you are analyzing. If you do, you might end up out of alignment with the writer's intentions. Remember that stories are told one scene at a time, so script analysis must take place on a scene-by-scene basis.
4. *Includes everything the character is doing in the scene.* For an accurate rendering of Step One, you must include *everything* the

character says and does in the scene. The literal step acts as a *common denominator* that answers the question, "What is the one thing the character is consistently doing throughout the scene?" All the individual moments in the scene must express the common denominator and vice versa.

5. *Does not need to follow the rules of action.* Step One needs to be *accurate.* Actability is not important because the actor will never play Step One in the scene.

   In order to find Step One, divide the scene up into smaller sections guided mainly by the dialogue. Look for where the conversation changes for the character you are analyzing; new elements can be introduced by that character or be in response to the other character(s) in the scene. By parsing the scene this way, you'll end up with a *list* of terms for everything the character does in the scene. Go through the script and mark where you think one section ends and the next one begins. (Example to follow.)

6. *Is stated in the THIRD PERSON.* This separation is not mere semantics; it reminds the actor and the director to separate the character as a literary construct from the physical action that the actor will play to bring that character to life. This brings us to Step Two.

STEP TWO: *What Is the* Essence *of What the Character Is Doing* in This Scene?[1] *(The Action)*

We have already spent a good deal of time deconstructing the nature and mechanics of a playable acting choice, but this step is ultimately the core of the analysis process because *the action is what the actor will actually play in the scene.* It expresses the deepest possible understanding of what the character really needs and how they frame the experience of the scene. Actions capture the *essence* of the scene, rather than simply reiterating the *appearance* of the scene, and thus they give the actor a *point of view* from which to play it. For our friend Michelle in the breakup examples, playing "put a loser in his place" could not be more different than "to explain a difficult decision." These actions, executed within the imaginary circumstances, *define the character.*

STEP THREE: *What Is the Action I'm Playing in the Scene Like to Me? It's AS IF . . .*

The As If is a memory device that helps actors to quickly identify with the actions they will play in the scene. In many cases, the imaginary circumstance of the scene may be unfamiliar to the actor – most people have not, you know, been the Crown Prince of Denmark, the President of the United States, or even a waitress in a small town in Texas. But actors can relate to the *action* they are going to play in the scene; the As If is a way to imaginatively understand that action in personal terms and how high the stakes are in the scene. It is also one of the director's most useful and efficient rehearsal tools to get actors to invest in, and commit to, their choices.

An As If:

1. *Clarifies what the action means to the actor.* Actors need to find a personal circumstance, real or imagined, that they can relate to in which they are doing the action. For every scene an actor has had some direct, personal experience of, there are a dozen that they haven't. Additionally, a good As If should not be overly complicated – the actor should be able to describe it in no more than a couple of sentences, with just enough detail to make it specific.
2. *Is not a "substitution."* The subject matter of the As If should not reiterate the subject matter of the scene. This may seem somewhat counterintuitive at first, but the director needs to get the actors' focus *off* the imaginary circumstances. The more the actors think about the imaginary circumstances during the scene, the less focused on the actual truth of the moment they'll be. The imaginary circumstances obviously come into play at every step of preparation, but to focus on them while playing the scene will often lead actors to *indicate* what they think is appropriate behavior. In choosing an As If, the important thing is not to recreate the scene but to imagine doing the action in a relatable circumstance. Also, the actor's version of the subject matter may differ from the dramatist's, and that could be a source of confusion.

   In our breakup example, let's say that the actor has chosen to play "explain a difficult decision" in the scene. She decides to work with a breakup As If because she recently went through that experience in her life. However, her breakup was far more vitriolic, closer in spirit to, say, "get a jerkwad to hit the bricks." So even though her As If is identical to the *content* of the scene, the *action* contained within her As If is completely different than what she is choosing to play in the scene. By using her version of a breakup scenario, she will be teaching herself the *wrong action*. To avoid this kind of confusion, and to get some imaginative distance from the scene, it is best to choose something completely unrelated to the content of the scene. (I think we've beaten the breakup example to death. We will now thank that scenario for its service and retire it for the remainder of the book.)

3. *Is purely a memory device.* The As If is meant to clarify the action and help the actor *prepare* to play the scene. Underline this next bit: *once the actor starts to play the actual scene, they must forget about the As If.* If they don't, they will be juggling two sets of imaginary circumstances while playing the scene – the As If and the scene itself. Actors cannot freely interact with their partners within the context of the scene if they are thinking about their own set of imaginary circumstances; it gets very confusing and distracting, *so actors should not think about the As If while playing the scene or their heads will explode like the movie* Scanners!

4. *Is IMPORTANT to the actor.* It can't be stressed enough that, although there is a certain amount of intellectual rigor involved, Practical Aesthetics is mainly an *imaginative* process. So, an As If needs to spark the actor's imagination. Great As Ifs speak to our fantasy life, to those things roiling around inside us. They are rooted in our longings and daydreams and should be employed without judgment. Anything that the actor would *love* to do or feels *compelled* to do has the basis to be a strong As If, but whatever the content, an As If must speak to something *truthful* within the actor. One of the most interesting things about working with As Ifs – and I've seen thousands of them over the years – is that you can tell almost instantly if it is meaningful to the actor. It's an inexact science, one based on trial and error, but when an actor hits on something that lights them up, believe me, you'll know, because it's absolutely thrilling.

5. *Has a cap.* Like an action, an As If should necessitate a specific response(s) from the other person that lets the actor know they have achieved their goal. Again, what's the tell?

6. *Is readily accepted by the actor's imagination.* As Ifs do not have to have actually occurred in the actor's life, but they should be within

the realm of possibility, however extreme. The As If should also be something that *is* happening or *could* happen. Substitution of the fiction of the scene for another fiction in the As If that is equally foreign to the actor does not give the actor an active, easily understood personal connection to the action they are going to play. Again, I refer to the notion of wish fulfillment and daydreams, those things we would like to express to the people in our lives but, for various reasons, do not. There is great power and vulnerability in making choices that are rooted in an actor's personal truth.

7. *Should not be too far in the past or have been resolved long ago.* Allow me a moment to draw a comparison between Practical Aesthetics and a traditional, Method-based approach to acting that utilizes the set of techniques that falls under the category of "emotional memory." In Method acting, emotional memory techniques demand of actors that they recall something from the past that seems to resonate with the perceived emotional life of the scene. As we previously discussed, no scene should ever be reduced to a singular emotional state. But there is another great failing in this particular philosophy: as we age and (hopefully) mature and as our memories grow more distant, our emotional connections to our life experiences change. Resentment gives way to wistfulness or acceptance. Joy transmutes into longing. Rage, with the wisdom, grace, and forbearance gained by the passage of time, can morph into compassion. The memory of a happy family reunion might turn bittersweet if, over the years, life, in all of its grand and glorious unfairness, intervenes with family squabbles, personal grudges, betrayals, and death. (People – ain't we just too much fun?)

Human beings cannot force themselves to feel *today* what they felt at a given moment in their past, so from an acting perspective, it's best to stick with stuff more or less in the now. As we will discuss in the forthcoming chapters, for the director, keeping an As If more or less in the present is the quickest way for an actor to make an instant connection to it and, thus, the action that they are going to play in the scene.

8. *Avoids the mundane.* Life's minor inconveniences tend not to fire the dramatic imagination. Let's face it: a lot of our daily lives is boring AF. So stay away from the stuff that dulls the brain and

flattens the spirit. Like all of these guidelines and criteria, this is a fluid idea, but here's a way to keep actors true to themselves: beware the tendency to make a mountain out of a molehill. If an actor claims to be at the pinnacle of outrage because a friend owes them ten bucks, in the politest possible way, feel free to call bullshit and then guide them toward something more meaningful. Actors who make these kinds of safe, anodyne choices might also be avoiding tapping into deeper places in their own psyches. That takes a lot of courage, but hey, in the words of the great Jay Ward's *Gallus gallus domesticus* super-hero Super Chicken, "If you're afraid, you'll have to overlook it. You knew the job was dangerous when you took it."

9. *Answers the question, "Why must I do this action NOW?"* The As If should help engender in the actor a sense of urgency to accomplish the action. So, within the construct of an As If, there must be a pressing need to accomplish the action *now*. To give a scene more tension, writers say, "Put a ticking clock on it." So, let's say the action of a given scene is "to boost a buddy's self-confidence." *It's As If my best friend, who has a fear of public speaking, is ten minutes from giving the speech of his life in front of thousands of people and he's sweating bullets.* The specific detail of the impending speech gives this As If a sense of immediacy. The clock does not always have to be ten minutes to go time, but the more urgent the need, the more the actor will commit to the action.

10. *Answers the question, "What happens if I don't succeed?"* Not everything is life or death, but because in every scene there must be something *at stake* for the character, there must be something at stake for the actor in the As If. So, the higher the stakes in the scene for the character, the higher the stakes should be in the As If. The answer to the question "What happens if I don't succeed?" needs to be based on clear *externalized consequences*, not emotional reactions. For instance, in the previously mentioned As If, if I fail to boost my friend's confidence, he'll make a fool of himself and lose his professional credibility. If, on the other hand, the answer to the question is something like I'll be annoyed or frustrated with him – who cares? It's just a feeling, and as we know, there are few things more fleeting, ever-changing, and ephemeral than our feelings.

Alrighty then! That's the deal on the three steps of script analysis. This process will form the basis of the director's approach to breaking down every character in every scene as well as providing some very useful directing tools that we will discuss in Part II.

Let's model the process with a scene from the Oscar-winning film *Good Will Hunting*. A brief plot overview: Will Hunting (Matt Damon) has a genius-level IQ but chooses to work as a janitor at MIT. After he solves a math equation previously thought to be insoluble, Professor Gerald Lambeau (Stellan Skarsgård) decides to mentor the deeply troubled, difficult young man. After Will is arrested for attacking a cop, Lambeau makes a deal to keep him out of jail if the kid agrees to get treatment from therapist Sean Maguire (Robin Williams). As the story progresses, Sean and Lambeau find themselves at bitter odds over what is best for Will, which is where the following scene occurs in the narrative. We'll analyze Sean.

INT. SEAN'S OFFICE – DAY

Sean and Lambeau.

LAMBEAU
This is a disaster! I brought you in here to help me with this boy, not to run him out...

SEAN
Now wait a minute...

LAMBEAU
...and confuse him...

SEAN
...Gerry...

LAMBEAU
And here I am for the second week in a row, with my professional reputation at stake...

SEAN
Hold on!

LAMBEAU
Ready to falsify documents because you've given him license to walk away from this.

SEAN
I know what I'm doing and I know why I'm here!

LAMBEAU
Look Sean, I don't care if you have a rapport with the boy – I don't care if you have a few laughs – even at my expense, but don't you dare undermine what I'm trying to do here.

SEAN
"Undermine?"

LAMBEAU
He has a gift, and with that gift comes responsibility. And you don't understand that he's at a fragile point. . .

SEAN
He is at a fragile point. He's got problems. . .

LAMBEAU
What problem does he have, Sean, that he is better off as a janitor or in jail or hanging around with. . .

SEAN
Why do you think he does that, Gerry?

LAMBEAU
He can handle the work, he can handle the pressure, and he's obviously handled you.

SEAN
Why is he hiding? Why is he a janitor? Why doesn't he trust anybody? Because the first thing that happened to him was that he was abandoned by the people who were supposed to love him the most!

LAMBEAU
Oh, come on Sean. . .

SEAN
And why does he hang out with his friends? Because any one of those kids would come in here and take a bat to your head if he asked them to. It's called loyalty!

LAMBEAU
Oh, that's nice...

SEAN
And who do you think he's handling? He pushes people away before they have a chance to leave him. And for 20 years he's been alone because of that. And if you try to push him into this, it's going to be the same thing all over again. And I'm not going to let that happen to him!

LAMBEAU
Now don't do that! Don't you do that! Don't infect him with the idea that it's okay to quit. That it's okay to be a failure, because it's not okay! If you're angry at me for being a success, for being what you could have been...

SEAN
...I'm not angry at you...

LAMBEAU
Yes you are, Sean. You resent me. And I'm not going to apologize for any success that I've had.

SEAN
...I don't have any anger at you...

LAMBEAU
Yes you do. You're angry at me for doing what you could have done. Ask yourself if you want Will to feel that way for the rest of his life, to feel like a failure.

SEAN
That's it! That's why I don't come to the goddamn reunions! Because I can't stand the look in your eye when you see me! You think I'm a failure! I know who I am. I'm proud of who I am. And all of you, you think I'm some kind of pity case! You with your sycophant students following you around. And your goddamn medal!

                    LAMBEAU

Is that what this is about, Sean? The Field's Medal? Do you want me to go home and get it for you? Then will you let the boy. . .

                    SEAN

I don't want your trophy and I don't give a shit about it! I knew you when! You and Jack and Tom Sanders. I knew you when you were homesick and pimply-faced and didn't know what side of the bed to piss on!

                    LAMBEAU

That's right! You were smarter than us then and you're smarter than us now! So don't blame me for how your life turned out. It's not my fault.

                    SEAN

I don't blame you! It's not about that! It's about the boy! He's a good kid! And I won't see this happen to him – won't see you make him feel like a failure, too!

                    LAMBEAU

He won't be a failure!

                    SEAN

If you push him into something, if you ride him. . .

                    LAMBEAU

You're wrong, Sean. I'm where I am today because I learned to push myself!

                    SEAN

He's not you!

Individual Moments for Sean
- Sean tries to get a word in
- Sean declares his competence regarding Will's treatment
- Sean questions Lambeau's accusation
- Sean tries to get Lambeau to understand Will's mindset
- Sean declares his intent to protect Will
- Sean denies being angry at Lambeau
- Sean tells Lambeau why he avoids him
- Sean calls Lambeau out on his pompousness and hypocrisy
- Sean tells Lambeau that his methods will severely damage Will

STEP ONE: *Sean is literally getting Lambeau to see that Will cannot handle the pressure that Lambeau is placing on him.* This is the common denominator of all the individual beats, assessed within the context of the scene. Even when things get personal between them and Will is not directly discussed, Sean's line of literal intent is always connected to making the case for why Lambeau's presence in Will's life is toxic.

STEP TWO: *To stop a narcissist from making a tragic mistake.*

STEP THREE: It's As If a cocky young martial artist I'm training with wants to enter a mixed martial arts (MMA) competition that he is nowhere close to being ready for. Why now: the competition is only a week away.

ALTERNATE STEP TWO: *To shut down an epic fraud.*

ALTERNATE STEP THREE: It's As If a business associate in the art world has been lying about having access to billionaire buyers. His lies threaten to destroy my business. Why now: we have an upcoming meeting with important clients and I know he is going to lie to them.

On the surface, the scene is clearly an argument about what's best for Will, but a deeper analysis suggests the scene is really about the long-buried anger and resentment between two middle-age men. Will is the catalyst that forces Sean and Lambeau to be brutally honest with each other for the first time. "To prevent a narcissist from making a tragic mistake" is a perfectly good action for the scene, but "to expose an epic fraud" perhaps speaks more profoundly to what the conversation really means to Sean and what he really thinks of Lambeau. Either of these actions can work. Which one is better? Let the actors test them out; they'll give you the answer very quickly.

Ura and *omote,* plot and story, literal and action: sensing a pattern here? Good. Now come up with As Ifs for those actions and another action/As If combination for Sean.

Beat Changes

A beat change occurs when the character goes from one action to another within a single scene. Knowledge of where one action ends and the next one begins is the key principle when parsing a script. The rule of thumb is that characters change actions within a scene when *new information* is introduced, of which they were previously unaware, that supersedes what has previously transpired in the scene.

For instance, in *Steel Magnolias*, M'Lynn's daughter Shelby arrives home for the holidays, and the two women spend a few minutes gabbing and catching up as they trim the Christmas tree. Finally, Shelby announces to M'Lynn that she is pregnant. This announcement completely changes the scene for M'Lynn because Shelby has health issues that make pregnancy very dangerous. So M'Lynn's action changes as soon as she hears the news; talking her daughter out of carrying the pregnancy to term is, obviously, far more important that having a chitchat.

The other guidepost is entrances and exits; very often the addition or subtraction of a character either carries new information or ends the previous action. Let's say we have a scene where a couple is saying goodbye to their guests at the end of a holiday party: "Goodnight," "Drive safe," "Merry Christmas," "Happy Kwanzaa," "Good Yuntiff," etc. As soon as the guests are out the door, the wife turns to her husband and says, "I'm worried about your brother." In this example, the first action is completed as soon as the guests are gone; the wife initiates the new action, creating a beat change for both characters.

In camera scripts, the sluglines (e.g., INT. COFFEE SHOP – DAY) usually delineate the beats of the story, although it's possible that the same scene might move locations; the conversation starts in the coffee shop, continues to the parking lot, the car, etc.

In plays, there are usually extended, uninterrupted periods of action between blackouts or act breaks. The director needs to parse these long sequences into scenes using both the new information and entrances and exits that change the intentions of the characters. (These are traditionally referred to as "French scenes.")

When looking for beat changes, don't confuse new information that creates an *obstacle* with information that categorically changes the character's need. The tension in a scene builds as a result of the characters fighting for what they want in the face of rising obstacles. Actors will drain the dramatic tension from the scene if they keep changing their actions to accommodate each new hurdle.

Multiple Character Scenes

When analyzing scenes with more than two characters, there are two essential conditions to factor into your analysis. First, you must identify in whom the *cap* of each character's action lies. Second, you need to figure out each character's relationship to the other, paying particular mind to those relationships creating either *allies or obstacles* to the characters' actions. Let's look at a three-character scene from the film *Coming Home*.

Coming Home centers around Luke Martin (Jon Voight, who deservedly won an Oscar for his performance), a disabled Viet Nam war veteran who becomes an anti-war activist. Luke begins an affair with Sally Hyde (Jane Fonda, another well-deserved Oscar), the wife of hardcore, active-duty Marine Captain Bob Hyde (Oscar-nominated Bruce Dern), who suffers from PTSD and a debilitating crisis of conscience over the morality of the US involvement in the war. Towards the end of the film, the affair now over, Luke comes to see Bob to help him deal with the trauma that Luke deeply understands from his own wartime experiences. Bob pulls a gun on Luke, itching to shoot the man who had been sleeping with his wife while he was fighting in Viet Nam.

In this scene, Luke's cap is in Bob (action: to make amends to a brother). Sally wants Bob to put the gun down, so her cap is in him (action: to convince a partner of my loyalty). Bob's cap is in Luke, whom he holds at gunpoint (action: to get piece of shit to beg for mercy). Luke and Sally are essentially allies in the scene thus they support each other's actions, whereas Sally is an obstacle to Bob's intention towards Luke. Understanding these dynamics will, of course, inform the rest of the director's choices.

Make sense?

A quick look at Marc Antony's "Friends, Romans, countrymen" eulogy from Shakespeare's *Julius Caesar* reveals that his cap is in the entire crowd, whom he is attempting to turn against Caesar's murderers. This example illustrates that the ally/obstacle relationship is often fluid and can change, often profoundly, during the course of a given scene. The crowd begins as an obstacle to Marc Antony, but becomes his ally by the end of the speech. The director needs to be sure that the actors respond moment-to-moment to the shifting dynamics in every scene, and be clear on the storytelling in terms of which characters succeed or fail to achieve their actions.

You must apply these two principles to every multiple character scene in order to be sure that all of the actors' points of view are clear, and that you are tracking the progression of the scene as it plays out.

Practical Aesthetics Scene Analysis Checklist

STEP ONE: What is the character *literally* doing?

This is a simple declarative sentence about the character that:

- Is noninterpretive.
  - Makes no judgment of the character's mental or emotional state
  - Speaks only to the FACTS of the scene
  - Does not factor in other scenes in the story, either before or after the scene being analyzed
- Includes everything the character is doing in the scene.
- Acts as a common denominator.
- Can answer the question, "What is the one thing the character is consistently doing in the scene?"
- Is stated in the THIRD PERSON.
- Does not need to follow the rules of playable actions.

STEP TWO: What is the *essence* of what the character is doing *in this scene*?

This is *the action* that the actor will play in the scene.

- The action is stated in the FIRST PERSON.
- A strong, playable action must:
  - Be physically capable of being done (accomplishable)
  - Have its test in the other person
  - Have a clear, definable CAP
  - Not presuppose a physical or emotional state
  - Not be an errand
  - Be nonmanipulative (designed to create order and is correct from the point of view of the character)
  - Be fun
  - Be specific
  - Fulfill the intention of the writer

STEP THREE: What is the action they are playing in the scene like to the actor? It's AS IF...

The As If is a situation derived from the actor's life that:

- Clarifies what doing the action means to *them*.
- Is not a "substitution"; the subject matter of the As If should not reiterate the subject matter of the scene.
- Is IMPORTANT to the actor, something that they would *love* to do or that they feel *compelled* to do.
- Should fire the actor's imagination.
- Has a cap like an action does – there should be a specific response(s) from the other person that lets the actor know that they are done.
- The actor's imagination readily accepts; it is something that *is* happening or *could* happen.
- Should not be too far in the past or have been resolved long ago.
- Avoids the mundane.
- Is used only as a device to *prepare* for the scene, not while actually playing the scene.
- Answers the question, "Why must I do this NOW?" (immediacy/urgency)
- Answers the question, "What happens if I don't do this?" (stakes/consequences)

Analysis Exercises

If you want to get good at script analysis, you need to practice. If you break down only two scenes a week for a year, if my math is correct, you will have analyzed over 100 scenes. Trust me, you'll be really good at it by then. So, let's start with Lambeau from *Good Will Hunting*, remembering to shake the Etch-a-Sketch and start over from square one. Again, it's important for you as the director to remember that each character in a scene must be analyzed *separately*. This is not a concern for actors, who are only responsible for the parts they are playing, but a director must have a complete structural and creative grasp of every character in every scene. Feel free to come up with several different action/As If combinations for Lambeau.

Lambeau

Individual Moments:

STEP ONE: What is the character *literally* doing?

STEP TWO: What is the *essence* of what the character is doing *in this scene?*

STEP THREE: It's AS IF. . .

Songs

Analyze the following three songs like monologues using the three-step process. Begin Step One with "The speaker is literally . . ." Do the same thing with the following list of songs or any other contemporary songs that you like but are way too expensive to be reprinted in this book.

"House of the Rising Sun"

There is a house in New Orleans they call the Rising Sun.
It's been the ruin of many a poor girl and me, O God, for one.

If I had listened what Mama said, I'd be at home today.
Being so young and foolish, poor boy, let a rambler lead me astray.

Go tell my baby sister never do like I have done
To shun that house in New Orleans they call the Rising Sun.

My mother she's a tailor, she sewed these new blue jeans.
My sweetheart, he's a drunkard, Lord, Lord, drinks down in New Orleans.

The only thing a drunkard needs is a suitcase and a trunk.
The only time he's satisfied is when he's on a drunk.

Fills his glasses to the brim, passes them around.
Only pleasure he gets out of life is hoboin' from town to town.

One foot is on the platform and the other one on the train.
I'm going back to New Orleans to wear that ball and chain.

Going back to New Orleans, my race is almost run.
Going back to spend the rest of my days beneath that Rising Sun.

Individual Beats:

STEP ONE: What is the character *literally* doing?

STEP TWO: What is the *essence* of what the character is doing *in this scene*?

STEP THREE: It's AS IF. . .

"I Wonder Who's Kissing Her Now"

You have loved lots of girls in the sweet long ago,
And each one has meant heaven to you
You have vowed your affection to each one in turn,
And have sworn to them all you'd be true;
You have kissed 'neath the moon,
While the world seemed in tune
Then you've left her to hunt a new game.
Does it ever occur to you later boy,
That she's prob'ly doing the same?

I wonder who's kissing her now,
Wonder who's teaching her how?
Wonder who's looking into her eyes?
Breathing sighs!
Telling lies!
I wonder if she's got a boy?
The girl who once filled me with joy,
Wonder if she ever tells him of me?
I wonder who's kissing her now?

If you want to feel wretched and lonely and blue,
Just imagine the girl you love best
In the arms of some fellow who's stealing a kiss
From the lips that you once fondly pressed;
But the world moves a pace and the loves of today
Flit away with a smile and a tear.
So you never can tell who is kissing her how.
Or just whom you'll be kissing next year.

I wonder who's kissing her now,
Wonder who's teaching her how?
Wonder who's looking in to her eyes?
Breathing sighs!
Telling lies!
I wonder who's buying the wine?
For lips that I used to call mine,
Wonder if she ever tells him of me?
I wonder who's kissing her now?

Individual Moments:

STEP ONE: What is the character *literally* doing?

STEP TWO: What is the *essence* of what the character is doing *in this scene*?

STEP THREE: It's AS IF. . .

"Chocolate and Strawberries"
by Debbie Diamond and Rick Boston

The night is over
Some woman's shoulder
You sit opposite me
Under mirrored ceilings

Club is gonna close in ten more minutes
I'm gonna give you five until then
If you wanna come home with me
Better pick up some chocolate and strawberries

Her dress is see-thru
I see right to you
Go-go girls are swaying
Foreign porn is playing

Club is gonna close in ten more minutes
I'm gonna give you five until then
If you wanna come home with me
Better pick up some chocolate and strawberries

Club is gonna close in ten more minutes
I'm gonna give you five until then
If you wanna come home with me
Better pick up some chocolate and strawberries
Chocolate and strawberry kisses. . .

Follow me down memory lane
Never to be seen or heard again
If you wanna come home with me
Better pick up some chocolate and strawberries
Chocolate and strawberries
Cover me in chocolate
Strawberries
Strawberries
Chocolate and strawberries

Oh, oh, oh strawberries
Chocolate and strawberries
Oh, you. . .

Oh, oh, oh, you

Individual Moments:

STEP ONE: What is the character *literally* doing?

STEP TWO: What is the *essence* of what the character is doing *in this scene*?

STEP THREE: It's AS IF. . .

Songs to Analyze
1. "Love to Love You Baby." by Peter Bellotte, Giorgio Moroder, and Donna Summer (Donna Summer)
2. "What Do You Mean?" by Justin Bieber
3. "Folsom Prison Blues" by Johnny Cash
4. "Norman fucking Rockwell" by Lana Del Rey
5. "Like a Rolling Stone" by Bob Dylan
6. "Bad Guy" by Billie Eilish
7. "This is America" by Childish Gambino
8. "Captain Jack" by Billy Joel
9. "This Land is Your Land" by Woody Guthrie
10. "I Can't Breathe" by H.E.R.
11. "Cross Road Blues" by Robert Johnson
12. "m.A.A.d City" by Kendrick Lamar
13. "I Am the Walrus" by John Lennon and Paul McCartney (The Beatles)
14. "Adelaide's Lament" by Frank Loesser (from *Guys and Dolls*)
15. "Hollywood's Bleeding" by Post Malone
16. "Big Yellow Taxi" by Joni Mitchell
17. "Not Ready to Make Nice" by Martie Maguire, Natalie Maines, Emily Robison, and Dan Wilson (The Chicks)
18. "Burn" by Lin-Manuel Miranda (from *Hamilton*)
19. "Landslide" by Stevie Nicks and Lindsey Buckingham (Fleetwood Mac)
20. "Stairway to Heaven" by Jimmy Page and Robert Plant (Led Zeppelin)
21. "Jolene" by Dolly Parton

22. "Sign o' the Times" by Prince
23. "Fight the Power" by Carlton Ridenhour, Eric Sadler, Hank Boxley, and Keith Boxley (Public Enemy)
24. "Disturbia" by Rihanna
25. "Thunder Road" by Bruce Springsteen
26. "Everyday People" by Sly Stone
27. "Watermelon Sugar High" by Harry Styles
28. "Mirrorball" by Taylor Swift
29. "Strawberry Bubblegum" by Justin Timberlake
30. "Won't Get Fooled Again" by Pete Townsend (The Who)

Notes

1 This checklist is fully explained in Chapter 3. Hopefully you read it and loved it.

Works Cited

Bettelheim, Bruno. *The Uses of Enchantment.* New York, Vintage Books, 1989.
Brook, Peter. *The Empty Space.* London, Penguin Books, 2008.
Bruder, Melissa. *A Practical Handbook for the Actor.* New York, Vintage Books, 1986.
Coming Home. Directed by Hal Ashby. United Artists, 1978.
Good Will Hunting. Directed by Gus Van Sant. Miramax, 1997.
The Januaries (Debbie Diamond and Rick Boston). "Chocolate and Strawberries." *Chocolate and Strawberries*, 2001.

5
THROUGH-LINE ANALYSIS

No matter the style and subject matter, every character is driven by a larger need that is universal to the human condition. Each character's journey, whether the hero or a supporting character, is in the service of trying to fulfill that larger, primal human desire that may or may not be directly stated in the story. Regarding a story's protagonist, this desire is almost always something that is lacking in the character's life at the beginning of the story, whether they know it or not. To further understand the importance of a character having a deep, unfulfilled need (even in a comedy!), let me lay a little basic psychology on you from a storytelling perspective.

The *shadow* or *"shadow aspect"* is a part of the personal unconscious mind consisting of repressed weaknesses, shortcomings, and instincts. Carl Jung believed that even though the shadow contains the darker aspects of human nature, it is also the reservoir of human creativity and imagination. "Everyone carries a shadow,"[1] Jung wrote, "and the less it is embodied in the individual's conscious life, the blacker and denser it is."

Every human being is composed of dark and light. Good and bad. The potential for compassion and cruelty. We are all, under the right circumstances, saints and sinners. Saviors and killers. Many schools of psychological thought suggest that at some point in a person's life, usually in childhood or adolescence (although in many dramatic stories it could be in adulthood), something traumatic occurs that creates an internal break. It might be the death of a parent (Christopher Nolan's *Batman* films), an act of horrific violence (the title character in *Tommy*, the rock opera by The Who), a betrayal (James Bond in the opening sequence of *Skyfall*), a devastating failure in adulthood that is never fully explained (Jake in *Chinatown*), or a series of events such as parental physical and psychological abuse (the title character in *Carrie*) or bullying (Chiron in *Moonlight*).

This event(s) is known as the *wound*.

The healthy human psyche manages to come to terms with its own particular iteration of inner light and darkness; it might be argued that human existence is a constant struggle to rectify these powerful, opposing internal forces. For many people, this is a terrifying, never-ending battle, but whether they know it or not, human beings make choices in life in order to heal these wounds. The choices can be positive or negative, enlightened or ignorant, self-centered or generous, but suffice to say, *a person's internal world influences the choices they make externally in their life.*

The journey of the protagonist in a dramatic story is an attempt to heal the wound.

Now, not every character in every story needs to be deeply troubled or debilitatingly neurotic, but on the whole, it is difficult to craft interesting stories about characters who are utterly content, self-actualized, self-aware, and lacking little in their lives. (Go ahead. Try it. I double-dog dare ya.) A plethora of American plays produced in the 1970s were about nothing more than, as Mr. Mamet once observed, "inconvenient things happening to nice people." I don't think any single statement has influenced me more as a writer, even when writing dopey comedies. The point is that a protagonist undertakes their journey in order to resolve an inner conflict, *whether they know it or not.*

When analyzing both a character's Through Line and scene actions, it's important to note their degree of personal self-awareness. Some characters are highly cognizant of the forces that shaped them and why they are striving for a particular goal. Others have a misguided idea about what they want and why they think they need it; a great story will provide a character with an *insight*, usually at the climax, that changes their view of what they desire and, by extension, their view of themselves. Because some characters are completely unaware of the unconscious emotional and psychological forces that drive them, their consciously chosen actions often work in opposition to their unresolved wound.

In the film *Carnal Knowledge* (directed by Mike Nichols and starring Jack Nicholson, Candice Bergen, Ann-Margret, and Art Garfunkel), Jonathan, Nicholson's character, is on a lifelong, unsuccessful hunt to find the perfect woman. (One of those women is Ann-Margret, but he rejects her too. Ann-Margret!! Man, there's just no pleasing some people.) But his relationships and abusive nature clearly communicate to the audience that his unconscious desires are driven by hatred and fear of women and a need to punish them at every turn. But if you asked Jonathan, he would say that he deserves to have a great woman in his life and why should he settle for anything less? The audience, however, knows better; in this case, they are clued into the character's inner nature far more than Jonathan himself appears to be.[2] So the director must help the actor make choices based on the character's degree of self-awareness at every moment in the narrative, especially since that level of consciousness will undoubtedly change scene-to-scene as the story progresses. In any case, the problem the hero attempts to solve in the story is a manifestation of the larger problem(s) they are struggling with *internally*, within their own soul, whether or not the audience is privy to the source(s) of the wound or the traumatic event(s) that pre-date the beginning of the narrative.

Here are a few more examples of wounded characters in film and theatre:

- Will Munny (*Unforgiven*)
- Harry Potter
- Aileen Wuornos (*Monster*)
- Becca Corbett (*Rabbit Hole*)
- Captain Willard and Colonel Kurtz (*Apocalypse Now*)
- Charles Foster Kane (*Citizen Kane*)
- Rambo (*Rambo* films)
- George and Martha (*Who's Afraid of Virginia Woolf?*)
- Christopher (*The Curious Tale of the Dog in the Nighttime*)
- John Wick
- Ginger McKenna (*Casino*)

- Athos (*The Three Musketeers*)
- Suzanne Vale (*Postcards From the Edge*)
- Charlie (*Me, Myself & Irene*)
- Evelyn Mulwray (*Chinatown*)
- Bree Daniels (*Klute*)
- Mary Tyrone (*Long Day's Journey Into Night*)
- Blanche DuBois (*A Streetcar Named Desire*)
- Eddie Carbone (*A View From the Bridge*)
- Alan Strang (*Equus*)
- Arnold Beckoff (*Torch Song Trilogy*)
- Paul (*Six Degrees of Separation*)
- The Wingfield family (*The Glass Menagerie*)

The Primal Need

The Primal Need informs the analysis of an entire character. Whatever a character – the protagonist in particular – wants will be dramatically more engaging and effective if it stems from a Primal Need: something universal and human that also reflects the character's shadow or wound. The journey the protagonist undertakes is in service of the Primal Need; it's largely in the writing, but the director needs to pinpoint the life force that drives the character forward.

Here are a few examples of Primal Needs; note that they need not always be one word.

1. Survival
2. Protection of loved ones/community
3. Sex/lust
4. Power
5. Love
6. Success
7. Wealth
8. Revenge
9. Fear of death
10. Relationships/connection
11. Honor

12. Reconciliation
13. Self-respect
14. Freedom
15. Fear of humiliation
16. Fear of abandonment
17. Justice
18. Fame
19. Acceptance
20. To prove one's manhood
21. Spiritual redemption
22. Closeness to God
23. Pleasure
24. Bliss/joy
25. Peace of mind

Examples of Primal Needs
- To save one's family (*Die Hard, Taken, Finding Nemo*)
- To protect one's home/community (*Home Alone, Straw Dogs, Taps, Black Panther*)
- True love (*Eternal Sunshine of the Spotless Mind, Wall-E, When Harry Met Sally, Splash, Secretary*)
- Survival (*Midnight Express, Nightmare on Elm Street, Schindler's List, Friday the 13th*)
- Freedom (*Braveheart, The Patriot, One Flew Over the Cuckoo's Nest, Gandhi*)
- Justice (*L.A. Confidential, Born on the Fourth of July, 12 Angry Men, Mississippi Burning, . . . And Justice For All, Munich*)
- Fame/notoriety (*A Star Is Born, The Lady Eve, This Is Spinal Tap*)
- Success/wealth (*Scarface, Wall Street, How to Succeed in Business Without Really Trying*)
- Revenge (*John Wick, Django Unchained, The First Wives Club*)
- Self-determination (*Dirty Dancing, Into the Wild, Eat Pray Love, Wild Strawberries, The Glass Menagerie*)
- To build a community (*Oklahoma!, Judas and the Black Messiah, One Night in Miami, Battlestar Galactica, Exodus*)

It's important to note that even for a story's antagonist or otherwise "negative" characters, the primal need must be POSITIVE. As we previously discussed – no matter how immoral, misguided, out of adjustment to reality, or otherwise prone to poor judgment we may think them – *all characters are acting correctly from their point of view.*

The Through Line

Simply put, the *Through Line* is the character's OVERALL ACTION, the thing they are striving to achieve throughout the entire story. Over the years, this concept has gone by many names – Through Line, Super Objective, Overall Action – different names for essentially the same thing. For the sake of simplicity, we'll stick with Through Line.

Here's a real-life (but totally made up) example of a Through Line: a day in the life of a bodybuilder.

We'll call him Arnold.

Arnold's Through Line for the day is "to prepare for a life-changing competition."

Here's what Arnold did all day:

1. Upon waking, 20 minutes of yoga stretches
2. Ate breakfast and took nutrition supplements
3. Drove to the gym
4. Worked out for two hours with weights
5. Had a chocolate protein shake
6. Worked out for two hours with weights
7. Had a vanilla protein shake
8. Consulted with his personal trainer
9. Had a massage
10. Had a strawberry protein shake
11. Practiced his posing routine with his choreographer
12. Did 45 minutes of cardio
13. Had dinner
14. 15 minutes of meditation
15. Bedtime

Now, most people's days are not as singularly focused as a world-class, professional athlete preparing to wow the world with his epically buff physique, but let's look at how the example illustrates the main principle:

Everything Arnold does serves the purpose, and is a function of, his Through Line.

Make sense?

Now, at every moment throughout the day, Arnold is not constantly thinking, "I'm preparing for a competition, I'm preparing for a competition. . . ." (By the way, did you read that last sentence in an Austrian accent? I did, for some reason. Weird.) What he *is* doing is executing a series of specific tasks (actions) that will *serve* his Through Line. In the dramatic analysis of a script, these would constitute *scenes*.

Let's also say Arnold's best friend, Franco, is concerned that Arnold is pushing himself too hard, so Franco convinces him to go out clubbing for a night. Feeling like he needs a break, Arnold agrees, so they go to a club and get hammered. *Really hammered.* Hung over the next morning, Arnold has to take the entire day off from training. So that night of clubbing didn't help, right? It actually worked *against* his Through Line.

BUT. . .

At the time, Arnold believed that some dancing and a few Cadillac margaritas would benefit his training by giving him a chance to relax. In retrospect, he made a mistake, but at the time he thought his decision was serving his Through Line. So, when analyzing a character, we must look at every action within context of the imaginary circumstances and how it serves the larger goal.

Let's now take these principles into formal script analysis. Remember that you, the director, will do this process for every character in the story, one at a time.

Through-Line Character Analysis
Establish the Primal Need.

1. STEP ONE: What is the character *literally* doing *in the entire story?*
    a. Go through the entire script, scene by scene, and do Step One only. Be aware of *beat changes* that occur within individual scenes and parse the text accordingly.
    b. Once you've identified all the specific beats in the script, look at all the Step One literal actions as if they were individual

sections of a single scene and then do an overall Step One analysis, finding the common denominator as you would in single-scene analysis. (The preceding list of terms for Arnold the bodybuilder illustrates this part of the process.)

2. STEP TWO: What is the *essence* of what the character is doing *in the entire story (the Through-Line action)*?

   a. Step Two is the *Through Line*. It will act as a guide and reference point wherein you spot-check your individual scene analyses with one simple question: "Is the action I've chosen in this scene in some way serving my Through Line?"
   b. Just like you would in a scene analysis, come up with the ESSENCE of what the journey literally means to the character.
   c. The big difference here from a single-scene action is that a Through-Line action does not need to be physically capable of being done because the actor will never actually play it. It's broader and more conceptual and therein lies its utility as an analytical tool.

3. STEP THREE: What is the Through-Line action like to me? It's AS IF. . .

   a. The Through-Line As If is also broader than a scene As If; it can be an experience, real or imagined, that you see as befitting Step Two.
   b. Example: "It's As If I'm trying to create a tech start up with my best friend because he and I have an amazing idea for an app."

Through-Line Example

Let's take a classic character from literature – D'Artagnan from *The Three Musketeers*.[3]

   PRIMAL NEED: To prove his manhood.
   STEP ONE: D'Artagnan is literally trying to become the best Musketeer he possibly can be.

STEP TWO: Win a permanent place in an elite group.
STEP THREE: It's As If I am working toward taking my Fifth Dan test in Ninjutsu.

ALTERNATE STEP TWO: Prove my worth as a newbie in a pressure cooker.
ALTERNATE STEP THREE: It's As If I am working for the first time as a speechwriter on a presidential campaign and I am trying to get my voice heard to shape the message and branding of the candidate.

Utilizing the Through Line is a very simple process. Although each scene action must, as per good Practical Aesthetics analysis, reflect the specific values of the scene at hand, the Through Line acts as a coordinating guideline. In other words, you must make sure that the actions in each individual scene somehow serve each character's overall purpose stated in their Through Line.

Exercise

Get a script. Pick a character. Do a Though Line, then analyze each scene. Rinse. Repeat.

Notes

1. Jung, C.G. *Psychology and Religion* (1938) Collected Works 11, p. 131.
2. Watch this film. It really holds up. In fact, I would argue that, at the end of the film, Jonathan finds the perfect relationship. . . for him. It's tragic and disconcerting, but it is the fulfillment of both Jonathan's conscious and unconscious desires. I'll say no more; I hate spoilers.
3. By far the best and most faithful film versions of the novel are the two films directed by Richard Lester in the 1970s: *The Three Musketeers* and *The Four Musketeers*.

Works Cited

Batman Begins. Directed by Christopher Nolan. Warner Bros., 2005.
Carnal Knowledge. Directed by Mike Nichols. Embassy Pictures, 1971.
Carrie. Directed by Brian De Palma. United Artists, 1976.
Chinatown. Directed by Roman Polanski. Paramount Pictures, 1974.
Jung, C.G. *Psychology and Religion*. New Haven, Yale University Press, 1977.
Moonlight. Directed by Barry Jenkins. A24, 2016.
Skyfall. Directed by Sam Mendes. MGM, 2012.
The Who. *Tommy*, 1969.

6

THE DIRECTOR'S NOTEBOOK

If you're anything like me and you can't remember where you put your car keys two minutes ago, jotting important stuff down is generally a good idea, especially when there's a lot to keep track of. Part of the elegance and utility of this approach to directing is that all necessary questions can be answered individually in one or two sentences, but you will find that there's still a lot to remember, so you might want to write it all down, which is a polite way of saying *write it all down*!

The point of any technique is to make the doing of a thing easier and more efficient, and in the case of directing, it should also provide *clarity*. So once again, it's your job as the director to chart out a complete action analysis of every character in every scene. Your road map will look something like Figure 6.1.

Let's look at what's necessary to prepare to direct an individual scene, bearing in mind that all the choices and adjustments will, in some fashion, reflect the Unifying Principle and character Through Lines, both of which we have already discussed at length. Figuring out what is necessary to get each scene to play dramatically essentially completes the director's preparation.

Actions

Your job as director is to maximize the conflict in every scene. There are several key elements to achieving this that will manifest powerfully and, if

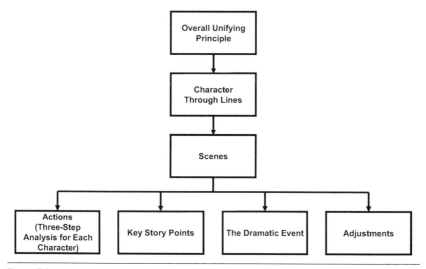

Figure 6.1
Source: Graphic by Jeffrey Eyres

the acting gods are smiling upon you, unpredictably in rehearsal. The fundamental concept here is to make sure that the scene actions *work in opposition*. Flaws in the writing notwithstanding, scenes often play soft and mushy because the actions, when juxtaposed together, are *in agreement*.

If actor 1 is playing "to demand an apology" and actor 2 is playing "to make amends for a grave mistake," the scene is over before it starts because the characters are giving each other what they want. Remember, a scene is a problem that each character, according to their best judgment at that particular moment in time, is trying to solve, even if their efforts seem ill-informed or misguided. Drama is created *organically* when opposing wills butt up against each other, so it's your job as the director to make it as challenging as possible for the actors to achieve their actions. In other words, feel free to make them miserable. They'll thank you for it later.

As counterintuitive as it may seem, the director's job is to make the actors as *uncomfortable* as possible. In your analysis of the scene, make sure that each action is as difficult as possible to achieve, within the boundaries of the scene.

As we will discuss in the forthcoming chapters on the rehearsal process, an actor will often chafe at being placed in a vulnerable position, but to get a truly authentic performance, the actor's understanding and execution of the scene must somehow mirror the difficulty the character is experiencing. (I refer you once again to the wisdom of Super Chicken: "You knew the job was dangerous when you took it.") So, place the actors as far down the rabbit hole as possible, knowing the obstacles you construct will bring them to life as they rise to the challenges of the scene.

It's worth noting here that there is a difference between *conflict* and *confrontation*. Confrontational scenes where tempers flare and the stakes are at their highest are often easier to frame analytically because the conflict is so vivid (e.g., *A Few Good Men*). But there are many scenes where the conflict is perhaps more subtle, even benign, at first glance. So, when maximizing the conflict in a scene, you must remember the writer's intentions and don't create a take-no-prisoners emotional death match unless it's appropriate to the material. You, the director, should not make things more difficult for the characters than the writer intended because it will rob the overall story of its natural dynamics; if every scene is played at a fever pitch of confrontation, the audience will cease to be moved and in all likelihood they'll get bored and check out. An old teacher of mine, by way of stressing simplicity and economy in acting, said, "You don't need to deliver a pizza with a 16-wheeler." Unless, of course, it's a really really REALLY big pizza.

A quick note on As Ifs: when they are employed as a rehearsal tool, the actors will come up with them on their own, but it's a good idea for the director to come up with some personal As Ifs that can be called upon as examples to help jog the actors' creativity.

Key Story Points

What, exactly, is a key story point? It's anything in a scene that does the following:

- *Materially advances the plot.* If we refer back to the beat change model in Chapter 4, new information is often introduced into a scene that moves the story forward. Ideally, every scene should somehow advance the plot by either helping or hindering the protagonist's progress toward their overall (Through Line) goal. If a scene does neither, meaning when the scene ends the characters are no closer or further away from their Through-Line actions, the scene either is poorly written or has no place in the narrative. Every director, at some point, will get stuck trying to make those scenes work. You have my condolences.

- *Reveals a new aspect of a character to the audience and/or the other characters in the scene.* Depending on how the narrative is constructed, the audience may have knowledge of the story that one or more of the characters in the scene does not. Conversely, the audience might not know what one of the characters knows, or they may have been purposefully misdirected by the writer to hold a false view of the narrative, which the scene will amend. (You thought all along that the detective was trying to protect the witness, but it turned out that he was the killer. That sort of thing.) *Any* revelation in the scene is essential to the audience's experience, and the director's job is to make sure those moments are communicated to the audience clearly and vividly.
- *Creates major obstacles to the characters' intentions.* A good scene usually contains a series of rising obstacles, especially to the character whose action drives the story. Key story points often raise the stakes and the level of difficulty for the protagonist; how the character deals with those obstacles is subject to the writer's intention, the director's instructions, whatever action the actor is playing in the scene and the truth of the moment. But major obstacles must be acknowledged in the scene, otherwise the conflict will remain static and the audience will sense a disconnect between the story and the characters' behavior.
- *Flips the scene/story in a new direction.* These moments usually create a *beat change* in the scene. Any moment that creates, in any of the characters, the need to begin a new action in the scene is of the utmost importance not only to the scene at hand but to the overall story.

Remember when Darth Vader announced to Luke Skywalker in *The Empire Strikes Back* – spoiler alert – "No. I am your father."? That was, arguably, the granddaddy of all key story points, because it accomplished all of the preceding in one fell swoop: it advanced the plot, revealed something new about the characters to the audience, created a major obstacle to Luke's intention, and flipped both the scene and the audience's understanding of the entire story (two movies' worth) in a new direction. Not all key story points are this profound in terms of altering the story and ratcheting up the audience's emotional involvement, but even a small, subtle moment can have a powerful impact.

Good directors, especially those who trust actors and are mindful of their own impulses to overdirect, will tend to focus their energy on the key story points in terms of both staging and instructions to the actors. How many key story points are there in each scene? Beats the heck out of me. There could be several that form a series of rising obstacles or, as in the case of *The Empire Strikes Back*, just one big ol' whopper.

The Step One (literal) sections of the scene analysis process are an extremely helpful guide in terms of identifying the key story points, but bear in mind that every new literal section does *not* represent a key story point. Use your common sense and don't give a moment more dramatic weight than it deserves.

The Dramatic Event

After you have identified the key story points, write a paragraph or two that describes in vivid terms the *dramatic event* of the scene. Write how you imagine the scene playing out with the understanding that this version of the scene will change once the actors start rehearsing it. Give the scene a descriptive title, for example, "Sean and Lambeau have it out over Will." Be sure to include the key story points and how they affect each character in the scene. Nobody is going to judge your writing skills because nobody but you needs to see it. (For that matter, nobody needs to see anything in your notebook. That's *your* stuff. None of their beeswax.)

This synopsis will help you envision the overall flow of the scene and highlight the moments that are essential to the narrative. It will also give you some useful reminders of where to concentrate your efforts in terms of instructing the actors, suggesting staging possibilities, and opening some other creative avenues not on the page. Pay particular mind to defining the beginning, end, and climatic moment(s) of the scene. (The latter is not necessarily the most "emotional" moment, but rather, the moment that has the greatest effect on the overall narrative.) The *Good Will Hunting* scene might go something like this:

Already in the midst of a heated argument, Lambeau tries to dominate the conversation, barely letting a frustrated Sean get a word in. Lambeau rakes Sean over the coals over his various screwups with Will, until Sean forces his way into the conversation. Sean tries to get the stubborn Lambeau to understand who Will really is and get it through Lambeau's thick skull that Will is at a dangerously vulnerable emotional place. Lambeau dismisses Sean's concerns as just so much psychobabble. Sean then really lays into Lambeau over his massive ego and exploitation of his students . . .

You get the idea.

God is in the Details: Adjustments and Notes

In the next section of the book, we will look at how to effectively give actors adjustments using vocabulary that is actable and clear. It is impossible to predict exactly what acting adjustments will be needed until you are knee-deep in the rehearsal process, but in the meantime, here are a few other issues to consider in your scene-by-scene preparation:

1. *Costumes.* Beyond circumstance-driven considerations like time period, location, time of year, the character's economic means, job, etc., costume choices must be expressive of the *action* being played in the scene. Consider a lawyer in a meeting in a glass-walled conference room with the senior partners of an elite "white shoe" law firm. In scenario 1, the action is "to persuade superiors to grant me their unequivocal trust." In scenario 2, the action is "to force slimeballs to admit defeat." Based on those actions, how would the costume choices differ in each scene? There's no definitive answer, but whether subtle or overt, the choices should provide a visual expression of the character's intention, which will lead the audience to draw conclusions about the character's state of mind. A good costume goes a long way in telling the story, but the choice must be specific and action-based. Obviously, you will (hopefully) have the talent and expertise of a costume designer at your disposal, but you have to think in terms of what your choices will communicate to the audience. It is, by the way, an

old truism among actors that a good costume does half the work. (The great Peter Falk modestly credited his multiple Emmys for playing the brilliant detective Columbo to his rumpled, now-iconic raincoat.)

2. *External adjustments.* Overall character externals such as an accent or a big physical change should be learned and habitualized by the actor as quickly as possible so they will not distract or make the actor self-conscious. Certain externals are required by the text and are essential to the audience's full engagement in the story, also known as *the willing suspension of disbelief.* Anything an actor does that does not appear to be an authentic expression of the story, such as an anachronism or other noticeable inaccuracies, will pull the audience out of its vicarious involvement in the imaginary circumstances.

If the character is, say, a cowboy born and raised in the Texas panhandle, but the actor sounds like they're from the Scottish Highlands, well, you've got problems. It's incumbent on actors to work outside of rehearsals to perfect whatever externals they wish to perform, but the director must demand that the externals are credible and seamless. This also includes physical states, which usually occur scene to scene, like being drunk or in pain. So, you might have a note like, "Bill got in a fistfight in the previous scene. When he enters, his face should be bruised and swollen, and he should be in pain from a broken rib."

Costumes and makeup will do part of the job in conveying this circumstance, but the actor must carry the ball as well through physical and vocal adjustments. (Please remember, should your fervent quest for verisimilitude begin to lead you astray, the actors don't need to be in actual pain; their job is to convey the *illusion.*) Please be sure that externals, whether specifically demanded by the text or of the actor's invention, are necessary to tell the story; superfluous external additions ultimately do no more than distract the audience.

Research

It is incumbent on directors to know their stuff regarding the text. You must be the master of your domain, so to speak. You need to know what every word means, including jargon, technical terms, and arcane language in which common words often have different meanings. Be sure you know how to pronounce all words and names correctly because you'll look like a doofus if you don't.

It's also important to have a strong grasp of the cultural forces that shaped the play and their basis in reality, but that comes with a huge caveat. Indulge me once more in a personal anecdote to illustrate the point.

Years ago, I acted in a well-received play in New York about a crumbling hospital and the people who worked in its emergency room. The *plot* was about the desperate efforts of the staff and administrators to save the hospital, but the *story* was about how people turn on each other when an institution to which they have devoted their lives is facing its own demise. It was a well-written melodrama, and the acting was uniformly excellent. (I played a doctor, which thrilled my parents and my grandmother, who innocently inquired after seeing the play if I might – in my early thirties – consider going to medical school, since I seemed to have a knack for it, and let's face it, it's every Jewish grandma's dream for her grandson to be a doctor.) In order to get a feel for the world we were to inhabit, the producers arranged for cast members to spend the graveyard shift in an ER in a Brooklyn hospital, which had recently seen its fair share of problems.

We saw some gnarly stuff that night: victims of violent crime, gunshot wounds to the head, mentally challenged individuals with nowhere else to go, and regular folks with migraines and tummy aches. We riddled the doctors and nurses with questions about everything from how to perform certain medical procedures to their personal drinking and drug habits; they were all surprisingly candid and helpful. One thing that struck all of us was that no matter how hairy things got, everyone stayed extremely calm. No raised voices, no backtalk, just a team working together with staggering professionalism. I had a private conversation with the ER attending physician – the guy who ran the place – and he told me that ER workers specifically train to stay cool under pressure and that he himself was particularly mindful of keeping it together, because if he lost it, everyone else's performance would suffer. I learned an incredible amount that night, not the least of which was that I had no desire to ever become a doctor.

At the next rehearsal, the actors discussed with the director what we had seen. What came up for most of the cast was the fact that the emotional temperature of the ER medical emergency scenes (the ones where we rolled in the crash cart and I got to yell "Clear!" before hitting the dude on the stretcher with the paddles) in the play was much hotter than the reality we had observed. But the story we were telling was about how individuals, when faced with losing everything they believed in and everything they had devoted their lives to, will viciously act out on each other in order to survive. The narrative, although realistic in many ways, took some dramatic liberties here. The director pointed out, and we all eventually agreed – some more grudgingly than others – that we had to play the *play*, not what we had observed. Our research certainly informed our work and made it better in many ways, but the director wisely noted that it was not up to any of us to impose "reality" onto the dramatic circumstances to the point where it distorted or, even worse, ameliorated the writer's intention. (Looking back, those ER scenes were super fun to act, and the audience *loved* them. So once again, go figure.)

Model Analysis

Now let's model the entire analytical process with a short play entitled *I Wanna Be A Spy*.

SCENE ONE

A nice suburban living room.

At rise: JEFF, 21, sits on the couch. Enter MOM & DAD, mid to late 40s, holding a cake with a few lit candles. They SING to the tune of "Happy Birthday."

MOM & DAD

Happy graduation to you. . . happy graduation to you. . . happy graduation dear Jeff-eeeee. . . we are so proud of youuuuu. . . !

JEFF

Aww. Thanks, you guys.

Mom and Dad sit on the couch on either side of Jeff.

MOM

Make a wish.

Jeff closes his eyes for a moment, then opens them and blows out the candles. Mom sets about cutting the cake and plating three slices.

DAD

I know you've only been in the real world for a day, but what are your plans, son?

MOM

Yes, you've not said a word.

JEFF

Well, I've actually given it a lot of thought.

MOM

Oh, that's wonderful! What have you decided?

JEFF

Mom. . . dad. . . I want to be a spy.

DAD
(laughing)

No, seriously.

JEFF

I *am* serious, Dad. I want those two zeroes. I want a license to kill.

Mom and Dad exchange a look.

MOM

What about veterinary school?

JEFF

No, Mom. My mind is made up.

> MOM

But you love animals so much!

> JEFF

It's my life, mom.

> MOM

But. . .

> JEFF

Please, mom.

> *She looks to her husband for help.*

> DAD

Well. . . okay then. We wish you the best of luck. We're sure you'll do great, son. Right, mother?

> MOM

Yes. Of course. Eat your cake.

> *They eat their cake in silence. Suddenly Mom viciously stabs the cake with the cake cutter, chopping it to ribbons. Pause.*

> MOM
> *(of cake, sweetly)*

How is it?

> JEFF/DAD

Good.

SCENE TWO

> *An office. Jeff sits opposite the DEPUTY DIRECTOR.*

> DEPUTY DIRECTOR

You test scores are impressive.

                    JEFF

Thank you, ma'am.

                    DEPUTY DIRECTOR

Do you think you have what it takes to be a "double-oh"?

                    JEFF

Yes ma'am. I do.

                    DEPUTY DIRECTOR

I guess we'll see, but it won't be easy. Most cadets wash out after a couple of weeks.

                    JEFF

Bring it, ma'am.

SCENE THREE

A training room with a padded floor, like a wrestling mat. Jeff stands opposite a female CADET. The Deputy Director stands close by, holding a clipboard.

                    DEPUTY DIRECTOR
                    (to Jeff)

Hit her.

                    JEFF

I'm sorry?

                    DEPUTY DIRECTOR

Hit. Her. Now.

                    JEFF

I. . . I can't hit a woman.

                    DEPUTY DIRECTOR

She'll defend herself. Or she won't.

                    JEFF

But. . .

                    DEPUTY DIRECTOR
Hit her!

                    JEFF
I can't. I was raised to... I'm sorry.

> *The Deputy Director nods at the Cadet, who steps forward.*

                    JEFF
Hi.

                    CADET
Hi.

> *She knocks Jeff out cold with one punch. The Deputy Director shakes her head, then makes a note on her clipboard.*

SCENE FOUR

> *Mom and Dad's living room. Dad and Jeff; Jeff has a black eye.*

                    DAD
This isn't for you, son. Please quit.

                    JEFF
No, dad. I'm staying. So I still need the tuition.

                    DAD
But c'mon, I mean, a *girl*...

                    JEFF
Lucky shot.

                    DAD
Tell you what: I'll pay for vet school instead.

                    JEFF
Dad...

DAD

And a car. What do you say?

JEFF

Forget it.

Jeff rises. Dad gestures "wait." Dad writes Jeff a check.

DAD

Don't tell your mother.

Offstage, a SCREAM like a banshee wail is heard.

DAD

She's still a little upset.

SCENE FIVE

The Deputy Director's office. She reviews a file while Jeff waits.

DEPUTY DIRECTOR

Well. I have to say: you surprised us all us. Top of your class.

JEFF

Wow. Really?

DEPUTY DIRECTOR

Really. Congratulations.

JEFF

Thank you, ma'am.

DEPUTY DIRECTOR

Now. . . to get your zeroes. . . you have to make your first kill. If you fail, you're out.

She places a HANDGUN and a SILENCER on the desk. Holds up a small folded piece of paper.

DEPUTY DIRECTOR

Your target has been selling secrets to our enemies. You need to retrieve the stolen laptop and then. . . neutralize.

                    JEFF
I understand.

                    DEPUTY DIRECTOR
Good.

                    She hands him the piece of paper. Jeff unfolds it,
                    reads. Pause.

                    DEPUTY DIRECTOR
You good?

                    JEFF
I'm good.

                    Jeff takes the gun and silencer, exits.

                    DEPUTY DIRECTOR
                    (to self)
We'll see.

SCENE SIX

                    Mom and Dad's living room. Jeff waits on the couch.
                    Enter Mom and Dad through the front door.

                    MOM
Honey! What are you doing here?

                    JEFF
Just came by to say hi. Hi.

                    MOM
What a pleasant surprise. You hungry?

                    Jeff pulls out a LAPTOP from behind the couch
                    cushions.

                    DAD
Oh! I've been looking all over for that. Good job, son. I'll take. . .

> *Dad approaches Jeff to get the laptop. Jeff produces the gun, silencer attached. Points it at them.*

JEFF

Why, you guys?

DAD

What are you. . . ?

JEFF

I was sent here to. . . neutralize you.

DAD

"Neutralize"? What does that mean?

JEFF

Kill.

MOM

Honey, please put that down. You're scaring me.

JEFF

You *should* be scared.

MOM

Jeffrey! I'm your mother! You put that gun down right now!

> Jeff lowers the gun.

MOM

Now please tell me what is this all. . .

JEFF

Get in the car and go.

MOM

But. . .

JEFF

Now. Otherwise. . . I have no choice.

DAD

Son, let me explain. . .

Jeff points the gun at them.

JEFF

Now.

Mom and Dad exchange a "yes" nod, exit. Pause. Mom and Dad reenter. . . followed by. . . the Deputy Director.

DEPUTY DIRECTOR
(to Jeff)

You probably have some questions.

Jeff nods mutely. Looks at his parents.

DAD

Son. . . there's some things your mom and I never told you.

JEFF

You work for the firm?

DAD

We do.

MOM

For a long time.

JEFF

Why didn't you tell me?

MOM

You get what the *secret* part means in "secret agent," right?

JEFF
(to Deputy Director)

So I guess I failed the test.

DEPUTY DIRECTOR

No. You passed.

                    JEFF

But I didn't kill. . .

               DEPUTY DIRECTOR

You were going to lie, tell us you did it, right?

                    JEFF

Yes.

               DEPUTY DIRECTOR

We really don't want to work with anyone crazy enough to shoot their own parents. So welcome to the firm. Your next job will be for real. And from now on, you'll report directly to your parents.

                    JEFF

I'm sorry?

               DEPUTY DIRECTOR

Your Mom and Dad will be your handlers from now on. You'll do everything they tell you to do, no questions asked.

                    DAD

Welcome aboard, son.

> *Jeff sets the gun down on the coffee table, rises, heads for the door.*

               DEPUTY DIRECTOR

Where are you going?

                    JEFF

Fuck you, that's where I'm going.

> *Exit Jeff.*

> *Blackout.*

                 THE END

***

I hope you enjoyed *I Wanna Be A Spy*. If any of you dear readers know anyone on the Pulitzer Prize committee, feel free to submit the play on my behalf. In the meantime, let's go through the entire analysis process.

OVERALL UNIFYING PRINCIPLE: In order to live an authentic life, one must break free of parental and other authority, no matter how well-meaning.

Analysis of Jeff

Primal Need: Self-Determination

Character Through-Line Analysis

1. Jeff is literally trying to become a 00 secret agent.
2. Through-Line action: To prove I'm up to the challenge of a lifetime.

Scene One

1. Jeff is literally letting his parents know of his plans to become a spy.
2. Action: To win skeptics' support for my dream.

Scene Two

1. Jeff is literally interviewing with the Deputy Director of the spy school.
2. Action: To convince a gatekeeper I'm the man.

Scene Three

1. Jeff is literally trying to get out of fighting a female cadet.
2. Action: To implore a superior to grant an exception.

Scene Four

1. Jeff is literally getting tuition money from his dad.
2. Action: To hold a mentor to his word.

Scene Five
1. Jeff is literally getting his first mission as a secret agent.
2. Action: To win a superior's absolute trust.

Scene Six A
1. Jeff is literally confronting his parents over their secret lives as traitors to their country.
2. Action: To force enemies to see that it's game over.

Scene Six B
1. Jeff is literally trying to make sense of the fake mission.
2. Action: To insist betrayers cut the bullshit.

Now come up with the following:

1. As Ifs for all of Jeff's actions.
2. The key story points, dramatic events, and adjustments for every scene.
3. A complete analysis of the other characters, including As Ifs.

Exercises

1. Pick a short (or full-length) play and do the analysis process for each character, including As Ifs. Be sure that you've maximized the conflict in each scene.
2. Pick a short (or feature-length) film script and do the analysis process, including As Ifs. This time add notes on costumes and other externals.

Works Cited

Good Will Hunting. Directed by Gus Van Sant. Miramax, 1997.

Part II
The Rehearsal Process

7
Early Rehearsals

In a sense, the real work begins when you, the director, walk in the door and sit down with your actors. Although the director must lead the way, they are also best served by creating a spirit of collaboration, inquiry, and openness to all ideas. (Except the really dumb ones. Don't waste your time on nonsense.) You have the final say, but the rehearsal process should be fertile ground for happy accidents and new discoveries. This creative spirit must of course be balanced against the practical necessity of getting the play on its feet or the scene ready to shoot. As I said in the Introduction, time is your most valuable asset and you must use it wisely. When rehearsing a play, you generally have the luxury of an extended rehearsal period, a feature film less so, and television is often run and gun. But the assiduous, detailed work you did on the script will empower you to function happily and effectively, whatever the circumstances or time pressure. Preparation is always the key.

The point of the rehearsal process is to create a set of *habits* in the actors that will enable them to play freely and spontaneously. The lines must become habitual. Playing the actions in each scene must become habitual. Tethering the lines to the actions must become habitual. Blocking must become habitual. Any external adjustments must become habitual. There's an old adage about acting: "You perform what you rehearse." So, your job is to make sure that each rehearsal serves to help the actors habitualize a key component of their performance. This is best accomplished one step at a time, utilizing the techniques and principles outlined in Part I. (Please read Part I first. It's why I put it before Part II.)

The first section of this book was devoted to giving the director some tools to create a working framework and a means of communication that will be easy for any actor to digest. Now we will go into much greater detail in terms of effective vocabulary, but you must remember that it is not the director's job to teach acting. You hired the actors based on their overall ability and suitability for the role; directors ultimately do not care how an actor achieves the desired results – if an actor's personal technique involves doing handstands and speaking in tongues, as long as it works, fine. So, good directors balances a clear-eyed view of the story while staying open to the contributions of the actors, who will inevitably surprise and delight them. (You do like working with actors, right? If not, go trade this book in and pick up another how-to book on something that you *do* like, such as bass fishing, home brewing, or Mahjong.)

I worked for many years with a very talented actress who at first drove me a little nuts because she never did what I expected her to do. It frustrated me because, as I discovered after some self-reflection, I was just too locked into my own ideas about the characters she was playing. Even her line delivery had a quirky, unpredictable cadence. But once I embraced her talent and uniqueness and allowed her work to help shape the play, directing her became a pleasure. As long as what she was doing somehow told the story, it was all good. So, don't dismiss an idea until you've had a chance to fully explore it in rehearsal. (Again, except for the super dumb ones. Don't waste your time. Sometimes it's okay to say "no" and move on.) Respect every actor's process no matter how they work, as long as they are respectful of you and the rest of the cast and don't waste time.

Your job as the director is to communicate what you want from the actors without imposing an acting technique – even one as effective as Practical Aesthetics – on the rehearsal process. As we will discuss, there are ways of utilizing the technique without forcing it on the actors; the vocabulary of action and intention is generally foolproof, so trust your preparation and work methodically.

Each rehearsal must have a clear focus and agenda. It's a big mistake to try to cram too much into one session, or to do everything at once. For instance, it's less than ideal to try to work out actions and the mechanics of the scene with the actors while staging and also giving line notes and addressing other minutiae. Even if you are pressed for time and have to get it all done at once, even in one rehearsal, *work on one thing at a time*. If you sequence your rehearsal process with logic and common sense, then each subsequent rehearsal will be built upon the previous ones, and things will come together organically.

Working With the Writer

We've discussed at length the parameters of directorial creativity and the practical concerns that arise. It is important to understand how the director's job differs when working with a living playwright or screenwriter on original material. It is not the director's job to rewrite the script,[1] but in a good working relationship between the writer and director, the latter should be able to make suggestions about what is and is not working. I knew a playwright-director team that produced many successful plays together, including several on Broadway, and they had a loose understanding: the writer had the last word on text, the director the last word on staging. This particular writer also understood that his presence might make the actors self-conscious, so he usually split for a while early on to let the actors and director do their thing. A very smart move.

Personally, I think the writer should be present for the first table read and then go take a vacation for a couple of weeks, preferably in some remote location with frothy, fruity cocktails and without cellular service or Internet access. Actors need some time to find their footing. A long-time colleague of mine, a terrific actress, once kvetched to me about the pressure the cast felt by the presence of a skittish, intrusive writer in the early rehearsals. "Doesn't he know everyone sucks the first two weeks?" she asked. Best for the writer to give the actors and director some space to get it together.

Conversely, when in the rehearsal room, writers need to respect the director's authority. They should never speak directly to the cast or give notes, other than to say, at the end of the rehearsal, "Great job, everybody!" Any issues should be hashed out in private between the writer and director, but the director runs the rehearsals. *Period*. I do not mean, by the way, to paint the writer-director relationship as inherently adversarial – it certainly shouldn't be. But again, there are professional boundaries that must be respected for everyone's benefit.

First Rehearsal: Table Read

First table reads can be anxiety-producing for actors. Some are keen to make a good impression on the other actors and the director; if it's a comedy they want to be funny, etc. This can lead to actors pushing for results, overacting, and making essentially uninformed choices way too soon. The problem with the latter is that if actors lock in right away, it can be difficult for the director to subsequently guide them in a different direction or get them to embrace new possibilities not previously on their radar. So, it's best to make the first read through as simple as possible.

Assure the actors that there's no need to make big acting choices. The purpose of the first read is to *hear the play*. What you *do* want the actors to do is speak up, speak clearly, and say the words *as written*. Ask that they address their dialogue to their counterparts in the scene, even if they need to read every word off the page. (Nobody needs to be off-book at this point.) At the same time, let the actors know that if they have an impulse or an idea they want to play with, they are free to do so, but make it clear that nobody is even remotely obligated to give a performance at this time. Also encourage the actors to pick up their cues so everyone can get a feel for the writer's rhythm. Read through the entire script without stopping for commentary after every scene. Just go from one scene to the next.

Be sure that someone – the stage manager, assistant director, your mom – is reading stage directions.[2] You want to keep the first read moving, so go through the stage direction reader's script and do some light editing; not every stage direction needs to be read out loud. Delete things like "cut to" in a camera script or any parenthetical adjustment to dialogue, like "angrily," etc. (You're going to cut those things anyway.) Just read out what's necessary for listeners to follow the scene.

After the read through is finished, it's time for coffee and snacks. This is a key element of good directing, so always make sure you've got some yummy, healthy stuff to nibble on. (And please: GOOD coffee. And half-and-half, almond milk, soy milk, etc. Not that yucky powdered creamer junk.)

Next, discuss some of the larger themes and ideas in the story with the actors. This discussion should be the beginning of making the story resonate personally for the cast. It also sets a tone for the rest of the rehearsal process, wherein everyone's ideas are valued, and says, "Let's explore this thing *together*." There's no formal agenda here other than to give everyone a chance to express their thoughts, ideas, and impressions. This is also an opportunity for you to share your vision of the story, and if there is a production concept, how it will affect the actors' work.

In facilitating the discussion, ask what the story means to the actors as individuals. There is no right answer; the point is to get the actors thinking about how the story affects them. Have they experienced something similar in their own lives? Does it strike a chord in them emotionally, politically, psychologically, etc.? How does the story resonate to the world as it is today? In essence, you are posing the question, "Why are we telling this story?" Get them to reflect on the opposing forces at work in the story. Feel free to share some of your own preparation in terms of the Unifying Principle, real-life examples, etc. Divergent points of view are fine – you're not trying to force everyone into agreement. Not everyone needs to be in lockstep about their understanding of the material, but there should be some shared sense of the nature of the play. Actors – and everyone else involved in a production – do their best work when they believe that they are spending their time on a story worth telling. I'm old school and don't want to rely too much on technology, but if you have audio or video that might stimulate the discussion, have at it. (Do not, however, show a video of other productions of the play. Bad idea.)

That's all you need to do for the first rehearsal: hear the words, get the actors relating to one another, and create a sense of fun and mission. With snacks.

Scene Rehearsals: At the Table

Okay – remember all the prep work you did that now resides in your notebook? Throw it all away. (Gotcha. Kidding. Relax.) Now we put into practice the work you've put in on the script.

Begin the first scene rehearsal with another simple reading of the scene. Encourage the actors to once again speak up, speak clearly, and direct their lines to one another with no pressure to "perform."

Now, every director has to find their own way here, but as we go forward, be aware of the fact that protracted discussion at the expense of actually *playing* the scene will quickly become counterproductive. Sometimes actors will, seemingly with the best of intentions, prefer to engage in endless discussion and deconstruction of a scene. This is usually because they are afraid. There are a million reasons for this, all of them perfectly natural and understandable, but none of them matter. There comes a time – the sooner the better – when actors have to throw themselves into the scene and see what happens. The anxiety actors feel about the scene is usually indicative of the fact that they have, consciously and unconsciously, begun to identify with the character's circumstances, and that can be unsettling. The following sums it up pretty well, I think.

From an Interview With Actor-Director Leonora Gershman-Pitts

Q: *What is the most challenging part you have ever played? What did you love most about the role?*

A: I played the infamous Hollywood producer, Julia Phillips, in the play *Inside Private Lives* for several years, both here in L.A. and at the Edinburgh Festival. She was bombastic, caustic, self-destructive, inspiring, vulnerable, and outwardly invincible. All of those contradictions were fascinating to discover over the years.

Inside Private Lives is an interactive play, and the audience was encouraged to ask us questions, challenge us, even argue with us. I portrayed Julia at the moment she was fired from her movie *Close Encounters of the Third Kind*. Before every show I would pace backstage, terrified and hovering on the edge of a panic attack. One night, our director, Lee Cohn, asked me what I was so scared of. I said, "I feel like the audience is going to yell at me. I feel like they're going to be mean to me and not let me speak my piece and explain myself."

He said, "Do you think, maybe, that's what Julia felt? The anxiety you feel about the scene IS the scene. It's all in."

That little bit of just-before-lights-up advice has informed my work ever since.

***

The good director recognizes that all those fears and insecurities are in fact the seat of great acting because therein lies the actor's greatest gift: courage in the face of fear. *Vulnerability.* In *Looking for Richard*, Al Pacino's documentary about playing Richard III, Mr. Pacino openly expressed his fear and trepidation about performing one of Richard's soliloquies, feeling that he did not fully understand its meaning and intent. He finally just said, in essence, let's give it a shot. He jumped in, and the results were wonderful. So be aware of when actors are feeling vulnerable. That's the best time to get them to play the scene. For actors, visceral experience will win out over intellectual understanding every time. But back to the table. . . .

Now the rubber hits the road, amigos. You have worked out the conflict in every scene, but your job now is to get the actors to focus solely on *their* intentions and in so doing lift from them the burden of making the scene work – that's your job. Actors should not dwell for too long on the big picture – it's actually counter to their best interests. Further, whatever actors say about what they want to do in the scene, or how the scene should play, is always in service of what they think is best for *their* character, God love 'em. You have to keep an eye on what's best for the scene, the story, and what best serves the Unifying Principle.

You must be clear from the get-go about where you want each performance to go. You also have to find your own means of expressing the ideas contained in your preparation, but I suggest that you avoid being too rigid and jargony in this rehearsal. Get the actors to dig below the surface of the lines and the subject matter of the scene so you can guide them toward a choice (action) that reflects what the scene needs to function dramatically and meets with your approval as being somehow true to the writer's intentions. Once actors have an understanding of that need, you can begin to suggest playable actions.

The first scene rehearsal should accomplish the following:

1. *Define character Through Lines.* Oh look: you've already worked that out. Good for you! As per your preparation, work with the actors on their characters' overall goals. Now, in this part of the deconstruction, the discussion of the character's "backstory" and

the need for an imagined character biography often comes up. Dwelling on backstory and the like can be counterproductive because it can lead to indicating, clichés, and nonspecific choices. Certainly, you want to look carefully at the text for clues; referring to *Chinatown* one more time, you know from what's on the page that Jake is somehow trying to put right a tragic event from his past by avoiding its repetition in the present. It might be a pleasant diversion to imagine exactly what happened to Jake before the story begins; it might even give some insight into the depth of Jake's need to protect Evelyn Mulwray, with whom he has fallen in love. It is helpful for an actor to imagine those events, great, but remember that anything that takes the actor out of playing in the moment is not helpful, so beware of these imaginary touchstones posing a distraction. In fact, any direction that takes the actor out of the moment in a scene is, how can I put this. . . *bad*. Dark Side of the Force bad.

So how can you help create a larger context for the actor that will inform the scene-to-scene choices? Your take on each character's Primal Need is very useful in this regard and can help actors understand the emotional and psychological engine that drives their character.

2. *Clarify the actions in the scene.* All that plot/story, literal/action stuff comes home to roost at this point. Focus on intention and obstacle. You might say something like, "Yeah, the character is trying to get a promotion, but doesn't it seem like she's demanding something that she feels entitled to?" Read that sentence again. (I'll wait.) Now, without being overly technical or dictatorial, you've just suggested a strong, clear action that makes specific the character's point of view in the scene. Go you! Once the actor understands the essence of the scene and has something of a playable action, you can utilize the As If.

Let's apply the As If to the character who wants the promotion. You've suggested that the real meat of the scene is about the character demanding something they feel entitled to. (A formal Step Two action might be something like "to demand a well-earned reward" or "to call in a long overdue debt.") The

As If can now be used as a quick, efficient rehearsal tool. Tell the actor to forget the scene for a moment and ask if they have ever felt denied something they worked really hard for in their own life.[3] "Yeah," the actor replies, "this one time . . ." Now have the actor do a little impromptu improv with their scene partner on the As If and then reverse to the other character. If the As Ifs really resonate, the actors will quickly, if not instantly, connect to their actions and start really fighting for what they want. When you feel that the actions are really living in them, have them go back to the scene. It doesn't matter if the acting is sloppy or all over the place at this point; what you are helping the actors to do is make a *connection* between the lines and the actions.

3. *Give a sense of the key story points.* After the actors understand their actions in the scene, you can point out a few moments of particular significance – the key story points. Don't demand that the actors nail those moment in this rehearsal. In the next chapter we will discuss how to give adjustments to get those moments to play. If you overemphasize results too soon in the rehearsal process, you run the risk of making the actors self-conscious because they will obsess on those moments throughout the scene, which will take them out of the moment.

4. *Get the actors to really talk to each other.* Good actors will focus their attention on their scene partners and react spontaneously and truthfully to their partner's behavior, according to the dictates of their actions. Even in the early stages of rehearsal, encourage this connection. Get the actors to acknowledge the obstacles of the scene, which, although driven by the dramatic circumstances, really come down to the other person's behavior. (This is why two of the hallmarks of a good action are the cap and the test in the other person.) Again, it's not your job to teach acting, but right from the jump, you want the actors to really get down and dirty with each other. Actors can't be polite or cautious or too reverent to get a scene to work – if they have chosen actions that tell the story, the actors have done their due diligence in terms of respecting the writer's intentions. Help them recognize, and

act on, *the truth of the moment* and then encourage them to dive headlong into the scene.

5. *Work on dialogue and stage directions.* Part of the actor's job is to be word-perfect with the lines by the time they actually perform the scene. This is obviously not a consideration at the beginning of the rehearsal process, but an old pro actor told me many years ago, "First one off book, best one opening night." So, the actors need to learn the lines *as written*. Many dramatists, in order to make their dialogue more natural, will include stressed words, pauses, ellipses, and half-finished words and sentences. There is a difference of opinion about this, but I strongly believe that those punctuations and stresses should be embraced because they will help the actors get in rhythm with the scene and discover some great moments embedded in how the characters are expressing themselves at that moment. But, bottom line, whatever the writer wrote has to come out of the actors' mouths. *How* the actors say the words is of course wide open, but they are professionally obligated to say what's on the page. We'll discuss about how to help the actors get their lines down in the following chapters.

Now let's talk about stage directions. Although it's much less frequent these days, writers often try to direct from the page via parenthetical instructions to the actor on how to say the line or, worse, what the character is thinking or feeling. Screenwriters call them "Rileys," a play on "wryly," which is just about most overused, and therefore most useless, parenthetical adjustment. Rileys can be as simple as a single word: "angrily," "wistfully," "joking," etc. Some writers get a tad baroque when writing these directions: "With a playful gleam that hides his simmering anxiety" or "From a place bursting forth deep within her soul." Okay, here's the deal: that shit is *unactable*. It will only serve to make the actors self-conscious. If the dialogue is good and the conflict of the scene is strong, actors do not need to be told how to say their lines or what to feel. So cross that stuff out and encourage the actors to do the same. It's worth noting that even great playwrights did it. Here's a stage direction from an early Eugene O'Neill play entitled *Now I Ask You:*

> Lucy comes slowly into the room. She is slender, dark, beautiful, with large eyes which she attempts to keep always mysterious and brooding, smiling lips which she resolutely compresses to express melancholy determination, a healthy complexion subdued by powder to a proper prison pallor, a vigorous, lithe body which frets restlessly beneath the restriction of studied, artificial movements. In short, Lucy is an intelligent, healthy American girl suffering from an overdose of undigested reading, and has mistaken herself for the heroine of a Russian novel.

I mean no disrespect to the great Eugene O'Neill, but this is nonsense. It might be somewhat useful as a casting guide, but try playing that the character is "suffering from an overdose of undigested reading." These kinds of stage directions were both the literary fashion of the times and a way for O'Neill, who began his career in the theatre working with amateurs in Provincetown, MA, to help his actors understand their characters. (The latter is my theory. That's all it is, a theory, so take it easy, O'Neill-heads.) So nix 'em.

6. *Watch for indicating or line readings.* We've discussed indicating: when actors attempt to *show* the audience what they think the character should be thinking and/or feeling. One of the telltale signs that an actor is indicating is the tendency toward *line readings*. A line reading is where the actor mechanically repeats the line the same way every time, with the same intonation and implied emotional content. It means that the actor is playing the moment in a preplanned way based on the literal meaning of the lines.

When you catch line readings, it means that the actor is either "in their head" or on autopilot. Line readings also create a barrier between the organic expression of an actor's truthful impulse and the line itself, so encourage them to just let the lines come out naturally without imposing anything on them. There will come a point where the delivery of the lines might be an issue, especially with comedy, which often demands greater precision in terms of timing and emphasis (or, if you will, em*pha*sis) to get a joke to play, but those are minor technical issues that are easily addressed. At this point, whether comedy or drama, help the actors rid themselves of their preconceptions and stay open to the truth of the moment. The dialogue will always sound more natural when approached in this fashion.

6. *Discuss externals vs. clichés.* As per your prep notes, first discuss each character's *overall* physical and vocal adjustments. Don't be overly demanding about the execution of externals in this rehearsal – you can lean into these things later – but do be clear on your expectations. (If you need to hire a dialect or movement coach for, say, a Restoration Comedy, arrange separate rehearsals that focus solely on those skills.) External character choices can certainly evolve over the course of the rehearsal period, but it's best to discuss these choices sooner rather than later because you don't want the actors to waste time and burn calories on stuff that just isn't going to fly. Also, look at any external called for specifically by the scene; if, for instance, the character is drunk, have a word about just how drunk they should be, how profoundly the physical symptoms should manifest, etc. A word to the wise: less is generally more when calibrating these elements in an actor's performance. But once again, the central question is, "What is needed to tell the story?" Which leads us to. . .

Clichés.

What the, shall we say, untutored actor often does is look at the character – king, queen, cop, cowboy, yoga instructor, whatever – and essentially boil it down to a template that is inevitably based on a broad stereotype. A king acts kingly; a cop is always a guy with a swagger; a cowboy walks bowlegged talks like a yahoo, and spits tobacco; a yoga instructor is forever in a state of mildly blissful Zen. But a generalized version of a king or any other character is a highway to that particular circle of hell reserved for really bad actors. Shakespeare's King Henry V could not be a more different human being than Richard II. The only thing they have in common is the fact that they both at one time had the same day job: King of England. So, when choosing externals, the actor and director must look at the specific needs of the character and decide if profound physical and vocal adjustments are necessary. But be aware, young Jedi: the more an actor leans into clichés, the less believable the audience will find their performance.

Externals are fun, by the way. Super fun. We must never lose sight of the fact that acting, for all its demands and the myriad techniques associated with the craft, is really the art of *dress up and play pretend*. Changing one's body and voice to suit a character is often a big part of dressing up and playing pretend, but we need to remember that everything an actor does, indeed every element of every scene, must be in service of the story and conspire to capture the audience's imagination and attention. Anything that reminds the audience of the artifice or feels imposed onto a character will piss them off, and their focus will wander to where to go for a drink after the show.

A performance worth noting that utterly dispensed with period clichés to great effect is John Malkovich's Valmont in *Dangerous Liaisons*. Malkovich, like the rest of the cast, retained his American accent, but spoke without any distracting, anachronistic American regionalisms. This alone was revelatory; with few exceptions, period pieces were always acted with an upper-crust English accent, even when performed by American actors. Malkovich's body language was also incredibly effective: he carelessly sprawled on the furniture, his feet up on expensive couches and chairs the likes of which one might see in the palace at Versailles. At first his physical behavior seemed almost comically out of place, but his work against the typical, cliché acting choices in a costume drama set in prerevolutionary Paris made the story come alive and feel vivid, accessible, and immediate. It also befitted the intentions of the character: the seductive Valmont was a provocateur, someone who defied convention and the expected proprieties of his social class, so Malkovich's physicality was spectacularly well-suited to the character. I believe his work also served to inspire other artists to dispense with clichés as the basis for building a character in a period piece. (It should also be noted that the Academy Award–winning costumes and sets certainly did a brilliant job of bringing the audience into the world of the story, relieving Malkovich and the rest of the amazing cast of having to carry that responsibility.)

There are no right answers here regarding externals, only your judgment as the director as to that which serves the story and that which distracts.

Conclusion

In most cases, you needn't feel that you have to solve all the problems in a scene at once. The first few rehearsals are really about setting up the targets that you and the actors will be shooting at. It is up to you to decide how soon to get a scene on its feet, but I firmly believe the sooner the better, even if the actors are still holding their scripts. So, let's jump to the next major part of the rehearsal process: staging the scene.

Chapter Review

1. Keep the first read through light and fun.
2. First rehearsal: discuss themes of the story.
3. Define character Through Lines with the actors.
4. Define scene actions with the actors.
5. Get the actors to pursue their actions.
6. Work with As Ifs to personalize the actors' choices.
7. Get the actors to really listen to each other.
8. Point out the key story points.
9. Watch for clichés and line readings.
10. STAY OPEN!

Notes

1. In Hollywood, directors sometimes rewrite the script without the writer's knowledge and permission; all I can say is, if you're going to do that, lawyer up.
2. In camera scripts, the paragraphs of description are simply referred to as "action." The same principles apply.
3. Avoid As Ifs to do with show business, acting careers, and the like. The desire for career advancement is laudable, but these As Ifs tend to run thin rather quickly and are very repetitive. And kind of boring.

Works Cited

Calhoun, Zach. *People You Should Know. . . Leonora Pitts*. zackcalhoon.blogspot.com/, January 20, 2015.
Dangerous Liaisons. Directed by Stephen Frears. Warner Bros., 1988.
Looking for Richard. Directed by Al Pacino. Fox Searchlight Pictures, 1996.
O'Neill, Eugene, and Travis Bogard. *Complete Plays, 1913–1943*. New York, Literary Classics of the United States, 1988.

8

BLOCKING THE SCENE

A major part of the director's job during the rehearsal process is to function as the audience's eyes and ears. It's the director's responsibility to make sure that the story is told with simplicity and clarity at all times and that all aesthetic choices conspire to give the audience the best possible experience. The *blocking* of a scene – the arrangement and movements of the actors in the physical space – is an essential element of theatrical storytelling, and it falls on the director to make a good job of it.

Blocking, by definition (mine, anyway), includes *all* movement in the scene – everything from perfectly timed entrances and exits, to broad comedic set pieces, to a simple cross, or to a subtle shift in a seated actor's body language. It's all physicality that tells the story.

The driving force behind creating the physical life in a scene are the actors' actions. This should come as a great comfort to you as the director because it means that your preparation is actually useful, and once staged, every moment in the scene will express both the natures of the characters and your overall thematic choices. Each character's action will provide a guide to staging for every moment of the scene and, when juxtaposed against each other, illuminate the conflict for the audience.

There are some obvious differences between blocking a scene for the stage versus the camera. Briefly, cinema has certain advantages over the theatre in terms of directing the audience's attention via editing and camera placement. We won't be discussing camera angles and the like (there are many fine books on that subject); better that we review some universally applicable principles in theatrical terms that will help you make choices that tell the story, create dramatic tension, and give the actors something fun to work with. You can, on your own dime, retrofit them to whatever medium you are working in. But at all times, your blocking must reflect where you want the audience to focus their attention.

On stage, blocking must always be precise and economical, otherwise the stage picture gets fuzzy and sloppy; when the audience is not sure where the focal point of the scene is, they get annoyed. This can lead to bouts of coughing, whispering, and worst of all, the unwrapping of hard candy, which in my opinion should be a federal offense. In the main, there should only be *one* point of focus at a time at any given moment in a scene.

Theatre directors differ on how much blocking should be done on paper before the actual rehearsals. It's fine to have some blocking notes regarding certain moments (especially the key story points), but completely blocking a scene in advance does not allow for the actors' input. Actors often have great physical impulses and ideas; if the director has planned out the scene with x's and o's like a football play and refuses to deviate, there's very little room for spontaneity and happy accidents. And to further torture the football analogy, most plays, even if run by a great quarterback like Tom Brady or Drew Brees or Eli "I got this" Manning, seldom go exactly the way they were drawn up on paper because, you know, the defense has other ideas. So, watch the actors: if they are connected to their actions and each other, they will often unconsciously come up with great physical impulses on the spur of the moment, which you, the director, can then go ahead and take credit for. Also, the initial blocking will probably change at least somewhat through the rehearsal process as you fine-tune the scene.

As we discussed in the previous chapter, the sooner actors get on their feet, the better, even if they are still holding their scripts. Many actors prefer to do the first blocking rehearsal script-in-hand so they can take notes. That's fine. Directors usually set an "off-book" deadline, sometime after the first blocking rehearsal, but feel free to annoy the crap out of them to get off book sooner. (Joking. Kind of.) Wherever the actors are in terms of knowing their lines, it's far more important at this point in the rehearsal process that they know their *actions*.

It's worth taking note of the fact that words (dialogue) represent a very small percentage of the interpersonal information human beings exchange and process. We respond to facial expressions, body language, tone of voice, and, if I may, energy on a much deeper level than words, although there's no denying that the emotional content that attends spoken language has a huge effect on us. But for actors, these nonverbal forms of communication are informed by their actions.

When first staging the scene, the actors don't have to go full out, but even when walking through the blocking they should be pursuing their actions, even if only at, say, Warp Factor Two. If they are simply mouthing the lines, there is no energy to work with, and things will seem flat and lifeless. But remember, you are focused on creating the physical itinerary of the scene, so this is not the time to give big acting notes. One thing at a time.

The purpose of the first few rehearsals at the table was to give the actors a chance to understand their actions and begin the process of adhering them to their lines. The purpose of blocking rehearsals is to help the actors adhere their actions to the physicality of the scene and to familiarize them with the particulars of the space (sets) they will be working on. Your staging will of course change depending on the type of space you are using. Here are the most common theatrical stage configurations.

A *proscenium arch* – the most ubiquitous in the theatre – is divided into nine sections (Figure 8.1). *Downstage* is the area closest to the audience, *upstage* the farthest away. This is basic stuff, but use proper terminology when blocking a scene so the actors are clear on what you are asking them to do.

A *thrust stage* (Figure 8.2) has the audience on three side of the actors, but the same terminology applies. When staging on a thrust, be particularly aware of *sight lines* (the visibility of the stage action to every audience member) because, depending on where they are seated, audiences in a thrust space have a much different orientation to the stage. Directors tend to change the stage picture more often when working on a thrust stage because they don't want audience members looking at an actor's back for too long.

In *theatre-in-the-round*, also known as an *arena stage*, the actors are surrounded by the audience. The playing space is essentially an enclosed circle. Sight lines are an even bigger concern when staging in the round. The directional terminology is that of a compass. This may get a little confusing or disorienting if your actors are not as well-versed as, say, a

BLOCKING THE SCENE 121

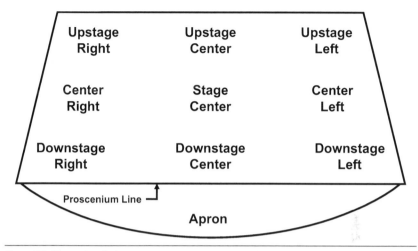

Figure 8.1 Proscenium Arch
Source: Graphic by Jeffrey Eyres

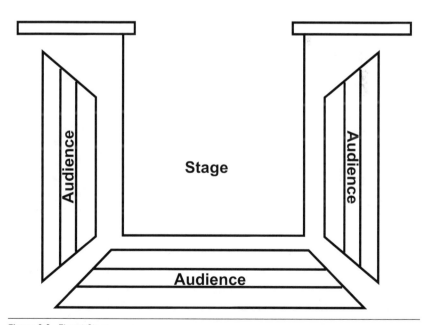

Figure 8.2 Thrust Stage
Source: Graphic by Jeffrey Eyres

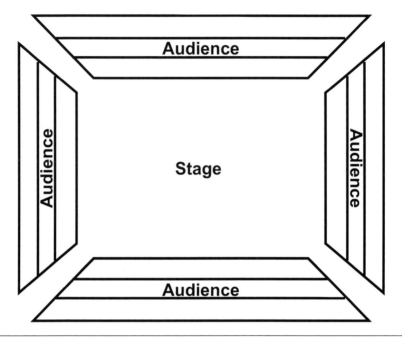

Figure 8.3 Arena Stage
Source: Graphic by Jeffrey Eyres

merchant marine or Star Trek's Mr. Checkov in the navigational arts. Some directors use a clockface, but let's face it, in the digital age, orienting to an analogue, two-handed clock might just elicit blank stares from your younger cast members. Whatever model you use, it's fine to just point your finger and say, "Go over there, please."

Whatever the configuration, it's your job to make sure that the actors *cheat out* and stay as open and visible to as much of the audience as their position on the stage will allow. Cheating out is a common theatrical term that means reorienting toward the audience so they can better see and hear the actor while maintaining the appearance of natural, normal conversation. Staging is a little schizophrenic (but fun) in that you are working on the internal dynamics of the scene while at the same time crafting it externally to make sure the presentation is artful and clear. But once again, as Super Chicken said. . .

Staging Principles

Let's start with the endgame: the physical flow of a scene should appear to be completely natural to an audience, even in stylized or heightened theatrical forms. As mentioned in the Introduction, the audience should never be consciously aware of any artifice; you want them to engage with the story and dream the dream of the play. Your staging should never call attention to itself, whether in service of a broad comedic set piece or an intimate scene where the actors never leave the couch. It should go without saying, but I'll say it anyway: *actors must adhere to the blocking*. Period. But if the blocking is fluid, dynamic, and makes sense to their intentions, they'll embrace it wholeheartedly because it will make them better.

1. *Using the key story points.* The key story points are a good indication of where to concentrate your efforts in terms of blocking, although you may of course have blocking at any moment in the scene that you deem appropriate. Sometimes a piece of staging might work best right before or after a key story point because movement at a crucial or otherwise telling moment of dialogue will often distract the audience. Let's say a character is going to receive some bad news in the scene. We can divide this moment into thirds: the director might contrive the staging so all activity ceases when, or right before, the bad news is delivered. Next, the bad news is delivered in stillness. Then, in the third moment, the receiver of the bad news sinks into a chair that you have cleverly and conveniently placed them adjacent to. This is not a fixed template; you can play with the timing and dynamics, but the point of the example is to make sure that key moments in the scene reach the audience with the utmost clarity. Remember that effective staging is always specific, and even something as small a putting down a coffee cup or folding a piece of laundry can, at the right moment, be powerful and revelatory. Or, conversely, it can diminish the impact of a dramatic moment.

2. *Actions and obstacles.* A piece of blocking should either enable an actor to achieve their action or create an obstacle. The great news here is that either one will bring the actor to life, although the more obstacles you can create, the better. As per Chapter 4, one of the key principles of parsing a scene is to maximize the conflict, which places the actors in the most vulnerable emotional position supported by the scene. Blocking is a physical reflection and expression of this idea: put the actors

in uncomfortable physical positions as often as possible. By uncomfortable I don't mean twist their arms like a Dutch pretzel; think in terms of placing the actors in positions that, in the main, make it as difficult as possible for them to achieve their actions. One character approaches the other to give them a hug; the other moves as far away as possible. A simplistic example, but action and obstacle are in evidence for both characters. You might also think of blocking as a game of *pursuit and retreat*, which changes moment to moment based on which character's action is driving the scene and which character has the advantage, however fleeting, over the other.

An awareness of the moment-to-moment relationship between action and obstacle will also help the director decide if a piece of blocking is necessary; anything that is not in service of an action is not essential to the storytelling and therefore unnecessary.

3. *Distance and tension*. Sir Sean Connery – a man who knew a thing or two about acting – had some interesting thoughts about a character's personal space. Sir Sean, who trained with the noted Swedish dancer-acting teacher Yat Malmgren, always worked extensively on his characters' physicality, as per Malmgren's theories of Movement Psychology, which explicate how bodily movement expresses the innermost aspects of human nature. One of Sir Sean's fundamental acting choices involved deciding the amount of personal space a character needs in each situation. Those in authority, for instance, usually require a larger bubble of space around them. It's not only a fascinating idea for the actor in terms of physical externals, but a very useful notion for directors as well.

Observe the way two people walk down a street: the distance between them speaks volumes about their relationship at that moment in time. Have you ever watched two guys jawing at one another, doing a "Come at me, bro!" number? (I have. More than once. Good times.) Forget what they say, forget how they say it, even forget their puffed-up body language. Look at the *distance* between them. If they both stay far enough away from each other to make a first strike impossible, rest assured neither one of them has any intention of throwing a punch. But if one dude gets up into the danger zone within easy range of the other, it's game on.

I observed a similar phenomenon in my martial arts training. Years ago, I had the privilege of attending a training seminar with Ninjutsu Grandmaster Masaaki Hatsumi, affectionately known to his many students and followers around the world as Sensei. He asked two tenth-degree black belts to come on the stage and demonstrate some sword fighting techniques. He handed each of them a *bokken* (bamboo sword) and they proceeded to aggressively dance around each other, faking and taunting, well within each other's striking range. Sensei watched for a few moments, and then told them to stop. He then replaced the bokken with two steel Samurai swords with *live blades*. Blades that, in the right hands, could easily cut a person in half. As soon as the black belts squared off with those swords in hand, they both leapt back about ten feet, causing an eruption of spontaneous laughter from the thousand or so students watching the demonstration. Sensei immediately stopped the exercise and pointed out that the live blades made the two swordsmen deal with *reality*, which expressed itself instantly in the recalibration of their distance to one another. Sensei then reminded us to always train mindfully and realistically.

Now think about staging that moment, but in reverse. (Go with me, here.) Imagine the swordsmen beginning out of each other's range and then moving *into* the danger zone. Imagine how that moment might impact an audience, when they suddenly realize that either one might strike the other dead. But in order for a scene like that to work, the scene needs to *progress* to that moment of tension where things become potentially lethal. The guiding principle here is that in any scene, *distance creates tension*. Actors like to be all up in each other's faces. It makes them feel heard, felt, connected, and secure. But in many cases, to put actors in an intimate alignment too soon is ineffective and counterproductive staging because the impact of that physical distance diminishes over time. When two characters get that close, it sets up an expectation in the mind of the audience. I don't mean to be crude, but before such things became politically incorrect, back in the day we used to refer to that distance as "fuck or fight." If two people stay close for too long without a payoff of some kind, the scene just kind of peters out because that intimate distance is rendered meaningless. Moments of physical closeness, whether benign or antagonistic, are usually more powerful when the scene builds to them, and there is some kind of pay-off or release of tension.

A great cinematic example of this principle can be found in *L.A. Confidential*, one of the best postnoir detective movies ever. Detective Bud White (Russell Crowe) visits "working girl" Lynn Bracken (Kim Basinger) at her home to, ostensibly, question her about a murder case he is working on. But what the scene reveals is that they are falling for each other and don't know how to handle it. There are several moments when they get tantalizingly close to one another, which amps up the sexual tension. At various points, one of the characters, feeling on the spot, will break away, but is then pursued by the other as the power dynamics shift throughout the scene.

Watch the scene a couple of times: you'll see blocking (and camera and editing) choices centered on the key story points, pursuit and retreat, distance creating tension, and two great performances wherein the actors struggle to accomplish their actions in the face of the rising obstacles in the scene. (The great writing also helps.) What's also worth noting is the *timing* of the crosses. Director Curtis Hanson wisely put the actors in the most uncomfortable positions possible at every moment in the scene, so when a cross or change of distance occurs, it has meaning and resonance. And yet, as detailed and specific as the staging and execution of the scene is, it feels utterly seamless and natural; Bud and Lynn are seemingly exactly where they ought to be at every moment of the scene.

4. *Crosses, positioning, and stillness.* A cross is when an actor moves from one part of the stage to another. It's not rocket science, but a cross can enhance the action or just as easily pose a distraction. Basically there are three choices when it comes to a cross:

   i. Line, then cross
   ii. Cross, then line
   iii. Cross *on* the line being spoken

The timing of a cross is important, especially in relation to dialogue. A cross calls attention to itself because movement draws the eye, so as a general guideline, it's best to avoid one actor crossing the stage when another actor is speaking. If an actor is speaking while they are crossing, have them walk in front of the other actors in order to maintain the center of attention. If an actor absolutely must cross when another one is speaking, have them quietly cross upstage of the speaker to avoid distracting the audience from the dialogue.

I'm not going to belabor this principle with tons of examples, but the main deal here is that you do not want movement to compete with dialogue because the dialogue will get lost. This of course does not mean an actor can't walk and talk at the same time – most human beings have mastered this intricate combination of motor skills, and it's perfectly natural for characters to do so onstage. These guidelines are incredibly malleable, but the larger point is, don't let anything happen on stage that will distract the audience from the focal point. On stage, even chaos must be carefully orchestrated so the audience can effortlessly follow every moment.

In terms of maintaining the audience's attention, remember that the director decides where the focal point is at every moment of the scene. But the actors need to have a bit of stagecraft and discipline to help direct the audience's focus. Ever notice what good actors do when a new character enters a scene? They look at the character who just entered. It's a subtle and simple trick, but it works in terms of guiding the audience's attention. The same generally holds true for dialogue: actors will generally direct their attention to the person who is speaking, unless they have a good reason not to. This is what we refer to in acting as an *ensemble*: a group of actors who selflessly support each other onstage and are dedicated to what's best for the story.

Even if actors are not directly looking at the speaker, they are still aware of the need to give them the stage. In fact, it's unnatural for actors to constantly eyeball each other as they exchange dialogue. People often look away from one another during a conversation, and at times may avoid eye contact altogether, so the director needs to position the actors so their faces are always at least partially visible to the audience, the aforementioned challenges of arena and thrust stages notwithstanding. If, conversely, you as the director make a decision to hide an actor's face from the audience, that's fine, just have a good reason to do it and a payoff of some kind (a new moment) when the audience can see their face again. When staging, think in terms of *angles* and *diagonals* because they are more aesthetically pleasing and provide the actors with the most visibility to the audience. Don't be afraid to tell the actors to cheat out whenever it's necessary. Sometimes moving only a few degrees makes all the difference in terms of visibility to the audience. Even chairs should cheat out!

All of the elements we've discussed thus far share the common purpose of directing and holding the audience's attention throughout the scene. Another helpful notion here is *stillness*.

Don't be afraid of moments of stillness onstage; they can be incredibly powerful, especially when juxtaposed against moments of greater physical activity. Great actors understand the power of *economy*. Sometimes the best direction you can give an actor is to strip everything away but the words and the action.

5. *Props and business*. Stage business comprises any physical activity performed by an actor, usually involving props. Business is either specifically indicated by the text or chosen by the director in service of the scene. Props and business, as functions of blocking, also serve to either enable, or create obstacles to, the actions being pursued in the scene. They can also help the audience engage in the imaginary circumstances. Business, especially in comedy, often works best as a counterpoint to the characters' actions. What's important is that you never add extraneous props or business simply for the sake of making the scene "interesting." Unnecessary business just clutters up the stage, distracts from the story, and generally causes actors to be diverted from pursuing their actions. Also, and this is very common, actors often like to be engaged in a physical activity because it makes them comfortable and, to be fair, gives them a sense of immersion in the imaginary circumstances. But remember: it's not the actor's job to

be comfortable, it's to navigate decidedly *uncomfortable* circumstances. In fact, their discomfort is the audience's entertainment! If a character is, say, at a party and feeling ill-at-ease in an unfamiliar environment, then sipping a drink during an awkward conversation is a bit of business that makes sense to the scene. It's also an understandable thing for a person to do at a party (so I'm told), so the drink might help the audience relate to the character's predicament. This might not be genius-level directing, but it illustrates the principles of telling the story, staying true to the circumstances, and supporting the character's intention. Now, having the character get sloshed and start stumbling around, if not indicated by the text, is crossing the line.

A great example of the use of props and business called for by the text is the tea scene in Oscar Wilde's enduring comedy *The Importance of Being Earnest*. Gwendolyn has invited Cecily over for tea so they might get to know each other. What begins as a friendly, charming exchange quickly devolves into a vicious competition when it's revealed that they are – so they think – engaged to the same man. In terms of staging, the ritual of afternoon tea – the dainty sandwiches and cakes, the elegant tea set, the lovely outdoor garden, etc. – serves as a comedic *counterpoint* to the growing enmity the two women feel for each other. Watching them try to maintain the decorum of the event via the physical business plays hilariously, if properly staged and performed with grace and specificity.

What this scene from *Earnest* also illustrates is the need for all physical business to be rehearsed to the point where it is executed cleanly and sharply, so don't be afraid of rehearsing a bit repeatedly until the actors have it down pat. Many years ago, some friends and I had dinner with Kevin Costner in Chicago, right before he was to start shooting *The Untouchables*. (Please do not contact Mr. Costner for verification; it was a long time ago, and I seriously doubt he'd remember dinner at Second City with a bunch of eager kids in a little theatre company.) I remember asking him how he was preparing to play Eliot Ness, expecting some deep thoughts about David Mamet's script, the character, etc. He replied that he was working on all the business in his scenes: he had to handle everything from guns to files full of papers at a desk, and so on. Mr. Costner said that he needed to work all that stuff out so he wouldn't be distracted. So, there you have it, and if you can't trust Eliot Ness, who can you trust?

6. *Physical contact, sex, and violence.* The first thing we need to be aware of here is that staging any physical contact, especially that of a sexual or violent nature, must be done with the utmost regard for the *safety* and *dignity* of the actors. These moments require the highest level of professionalism from all involved and also constant vigilance from the director to make sure that the strictures of decency and proper safety precautions are always enforced. Make no mistake: it's on the director to make sure the actors are safe at all times, both physically and emotionally, when staging scenes involving any level of violence or physical intimacy.

As we discussed, physical contact between actors carries a lot of weight, so choose carefully and specifically when and why the characters make any physical contact. Nonessential physical contact diminishes the impact of meaningful contact and often reads as sloppy staging. In the aforementioned scene from *L.A. Confidential*, Bud and Lynn *never* actually touch each other, even though they get close enough to inspect and irrigate each other's facial pores. This restraint raised the emotional and sexual tension and left the audience that much more invested in wanting to know how things were going play out between them. (No spoilers. Go watch the movie.) Conversely, if casual physical contact is appropriate to the scene and the relationship, great. Just be sure it's a conscious choice, because the audience assumes that everything they see and hear in a scene is somehow essential to the story.

When it comes to violence, the question you must begin with is, *what emotions do you wish to evoke in the audience?* A fight should reveal character, tell the story, and fit the style of the piece. The fearsome Hotspur in Shakespeare's *Henry IV, Part One* fights differently than the adolescent

Romeo. Blind superhero Daredevil fights differently than James Bond. What about two regular guys who have never been in a fistfight in their entire lives, such as the comedic altercation between actors Peter Firth and Hugh Grant in *Bridget Jones's Diary*? Jackie Chan, whose greatest influences as a performer are silent movie pioneers Harold Lloyd, Charlie Chaplin, and, in particular, Buster Keaton, fights differently than Bruce Lee did.[1] Chan's fights are usually, by design, outrageously comical whereas Lee's fights were all deadly serious business. The revenge-obsessed assassin Beatrix Kiddo in the *Kill Bill* films has an entirely different orientation toward violence than gleeful psychopath Harley Quinn.

Here are a few great fight scenes:

- The train compartment fight in *From Russia With Love*
- The hallway fight in *Daredevil* (Netflix series)
- The opening dance-hall fight in *Dragon: The Bruce Lee Story*
- The street brawl in *A Bronx Tale*
- The nightclub shootout in *John Wick*
- The hallway knife fight in *The Raid*
- The forest rescue in *The Patriot*
- The fight in the club in *Scott Pilgrim vs. the World*
- The martial arts fight in the Coliseum in *Way of the Dragon* (Bruce Lee and Chuck Norris)
- The bathhouse fight in *Eastern Promises*
- The back-alley brawl between the newscasters in *Anchorman*
- The final fight in *Drunken Master II* (Jackie Chan)
- The opening fight in *Kill Bill: Volume I*

I can now hear you, dear reader, saying, "Hey, wait a minute! What about that *awesome* fight in. . . ?" Yes, you're absolutely right – that's a great fight, too. We could do this all night. (Full disclosure: I'm a geek for fight scenes. Don't get me started. Oops. Too late.) The list is meant to illustrate various styles and characters, and the different emotions fight scenes can evoke in the audience. Watch some of them. Do you think the director and the actors accomplished the intended purpose of the scene? So again, what do you want the audience to feel when they watch your fight scene?

The same principles apply even if the fight only lasts for a few moments or is nothing more than a single, ineffectual shove. Whatever the requirements, you'll probably need some help, unless staging violence is an area of personal expertise – which means you have training, experience, and certification. So, get a fight choreographer and rehearse the living shit out of it so the actors are safe and the sequence plays cleanly, even if the fight is meant to give the *appearance* of utter pandemonium. And never forget that the emotions the audience feels begin with the performers.

For the actor, even though the rational mind understands that a staged fight or a moment of physical violence is pretend, the *body* doesn't know the difference, and often our lizard-brain, caveman "fight or flight" mechanism kicks in. It's also easy to get carried away, so again, any form of physical violence, from a single slap to a no-holds-barred brawl, must be staged slowly and carefully and rehearsed methodically toward the actual performance dynamics. The same holds true for sexuality.

Actors are, in the main, a pretty brave lot. They'll do whatever the role requires. But in the area of sexuality, there is great potential for exploitation, especially for women. So once again, it's on the director to create a safe space when working out scenes involving sex and physical intimacy. Let the actors know early what you are planning so there are no uncomfortable surprises.

A female film star once told my acting students a story about a film she signed on for that involved some sexual content, but no nudity. Her contract expressly stipulated that she would only shoot what was in the script, nothing more. Once filming began, the male director kept trying to get her to shoot a particular scene without clothes; she adamantly refused, so the director – a real piece of work – badgered and pressured her relentlessly throughout the shoot to do the nude scene, believing that it would help sell the film. ("Come see so-and-so naked!"). The film star, despite what she described as harassment and emotional abuse from the director, nevertheless stuck to her guns. Good for her! However, actresses who do not have this film star's power and stature might find themselves in an awkward, or even threatening, situation, so once again, dear director, *don't be a jerk*.[2]

Returning momentarily to the notion of a safe space, when staging or shooting a sexual scene, have as few people as possible in the room or on set. The actors must also practice good personal hygiene; in his excellent BBC special and book *Acting in Film*, Michael Caine discusses the importance of maintaining a sense of humor and the efficacy of keeping breath mints handy. As you work through the particulars of the scene, keep checking in with the actors to make sure they are okay with what's going on and give them agency to stop the rehearsal at any point if they feel compromised.

In the last few years, a consultant position known as the *intimacy coordinator* has emerged in all media in which actors perform scenes involving the depiction of sexual intimacy. An intimacy coordinator's functions include the following:

- Ensuring that all staff and actors are aware of the context of the intimacy as part of the story.
- Ensuring that avenues for reporting harassment are available.
- Making sure that the actors continually consent to all scenes of intimacy and all content therein.
- Making sure that all scenes of intimacy are performed according to previously agreed-to choreography.
- Ensuring that the actors mark the end of each intimate scene with a moment to signal the return to real-life interaction.
- Making sure that rehearsals and sets are closed and union rules are followed.
- Caring for actors' well-being before, during, and after "cut."

If all precautions are taken to ensure the actors' physical and emotional well-being, it will create a working atmosphere that will help them focus on the scene without fear of embarrassment or potential exploitation.

These days, film and television audiences find nudity and sexuality in film fairly commonplace and are, in the main, not shocked by it, although it can be distracting because we humans are still, so to speak, hormone-driven animals. I'm not prudish, and I have always opposed censorship in any form, but without going into graphic detail, I do think that nudity onstage can be *very* distracting. Ask yourself where the audience's attention is during a live performance with two naked actors on stage a few feet away from them: the scene or their bodies? Again, I'm not opposed to it for any moral reasons; it's just hard for a story (or anything else) to compete with naked bodies. Finally, beyond what is specifically called for in the text, it's the director's call as to whether or not nudity is in service of the story, whatever the medium.

In terms of aesthetic content, just as a fight reveals character and tells the story, a sexual scene should do the same. (If the scene is just there for purely salacious reasons, as is often the case in Hollywood movies, what can I tell ya? Do your best.)

Titillation aside, the actual physical act is really the least interesting and dramatic part of a sexual scene. Sex for sex's sake is just pornography. What are the characters' *emotional* needs in the scene? Do the characters need to express love to each other? Do they need comfort? Are they using sexual pleasure to escape their troubles? Is it a conquest? An ego trip? A dare? A mercy fuck? The satisfaction of crazy-making lust? A goodbye? A dream come true? A nightmare? These are the questions directors must analyze, just as they would any other scene. (Hopefully the writer has provided some clues here, both in the scene itself and contextually in the rest of the story.) Once you and the actors understand those needs and intentions, you'll have an easier time creating blocking that will be specific to the needs of the scene. Here are a few examples:

- The cabana scene in *Fast Times at Ridgemont High*. This scene is both funny and touching in its depiction of two awkward teenagers (Jennifer Jason Leigh and Robert Romanus) having sex for the first time. It also has a great impact on the rest of the narrative.
- The tent scene in *Brokeback Mountain*. Ennis and Jack (Heath Ledger and Jake Gyllenhaal), two gay cowboys who must hide their love for each other from the world, finally consummate their passion.
- The window smashing scene in *Body Heat*. Prior to this scene, Ned and Maddy (William Hurt and Kathleen Turner) have been bantering and raising the sexual tension to the point where Ned simply can't take it anymore.
- *Don't Look Now*. The graphic sex scene between a husband and wife (Donald Sutherland and Julie Christie) mixes intense sexuality with frightening visions of death and murder.
- The three-way in *Y Tu Mamá También*. A great example of a sex scene that changes the lives of the characters forever, especially the two young men (Gael Garcia Bernal, Diego Luna) who succumb to the heat of the moment (Maribel Verdú, bringin' the heat) . . . and each other.
- *Munich*. Deeply troubled Israeli Mossad agent Avner (Eric Bana) and his pregnant wife Daphna (Ayelet Zurer) make love as Avner tries desperately to forget the horrors he has recently experienced.
- *Bridesmaids*. In the hilarious opening scene, two lovers (Kristen Wiig and Jon Hamm) keep trying unsuccessfully to get in sync with each other in bed, although the dude keeps having the time of his life, utterly oblivious to he bed-partner's frustration.
- *Team America: World Police*. The hottest, raunchiest, and funniest puppet sex scene in the history of cinema.
- *Monster's Ball*. The intensely emotional love scene between Leticia and Hank (Halle Berry and Billy Bob Thornton) vividly portrays Leticia's need for comfort, release, and intimacy in the wake of a horrifying personal tragedy.

- *Call Me By Your Name.* The passionate first make-out scene between Oliver and the younger Elio (Armie Hammer and Timothée Chalamet).

Conclusion

Be aware of the tendency to make the blocking too busy because you thought it necessary to keep the scene interesting. As you refine the scene, don't be afraid to remove blocking and business that prove extraneous and unmotivated. Trust simplicity and economy.

The flip side is that sometimes a scene can get boring if the actors don't move after an extended period in the same positions. (*Sometimes.* Not always. As we previously discussed, sometimes extended periods of stillness can be riveting.) So do your best to find organic, motivated reasons for the actors to move if the scene begins to feel stilted. I would be remiss, however, if I did not mention that I've discussed this issue with many fine directors who have admitted that, once in a blue moon, at their wit's end, they said to an actor something like, "Cross behind the couch then sit on the chair." When the actor inquired as to why they were being asked to make that move, the director replied, "You figure it out." Hey, like I said, nobody's perfect.

Sometimes things don't work the way you thought they would, and it's okay to make changes. In fact, sometimes you might just get it all wrong or come up with a much better way to stage the scene. If you have an idea, try it. It's okay to change your mind! Just know that at a certain point, the blocking must be *set* so the actors can fully habitualize it, the lighting director can light it, the director of photography can film it, etc.

A fun way to begin the blocking process is to do a run through where the actors can go wherever they want in the scene: no formal staging, no concerns about sight lines, or any other presentational issues. Give them free rein and see what they come up with. The only parameters should be no sexual or invasive contact or violence. Again, those things must always be choreographed. *Always.*

Finally, it bears repeating that you must pay close attention to the actors as you stage the scene. Sometimes even the smallest physical impulse, when pursued, can grow into a great piece of staging and a great moment for the actors.

Trust your instincts! Have fun! Play!

Blocking Exercise: *Mad Men*

In the following scene from the television drama *Mad Men*, Don Draper, a compulsive womanizer who obsesses constantly over the women he sleeps with, goes to visit Rachel Menken, a major client of the ad agency Don works for as creative director. Rachel, a smart and self-aware woman, has been on to Don's manipulative ways from the start, yet the two share a strong connection, especially in bed.

For the sake of the exercise, let's block the scene as if it were to be presented on a proscenium arch stage. I've done an analysis of the characters' scene actions, but feel free to discard them and come up with your own. I've also suggested some blocking for the scene. Your mission, should you decide to accept it, is the following:

1. Write the descriptive paragraph and entitle the scene. You will find this to be very helpful in terms of helping you imagine some staging possibilities.
2. Define the key story points in the scene.
3. Block the entire scene on paper. (Again, for the sake of the exercise.)
4. Don't watch the actual scene from the show until after you've done the exercise. The point here is to imagine how *you* would stage the scene.

Mad Men *Scene Analysis*

Don

1. Don is literally trying to get Rachel into bed.
2. *Prevail upon a wise partner to relieve me of my burdens.*

Rachel

1. Rachel is literally trying to accommodate Don's unwanted and unexpected visit.
2. *Push a man-child to take care of his own damn self.*

NOTE: All text in bold is my blocking notes. The rest of the scene, including the action, is what the writer put on the page.

INT. RACHEL'S APARTMENT/LIVING ROOM – NIGHT

1960 New York. DON DRAPER approaches RACHEL MENKEN'S door and knocks. It's late and his boss has just had a heart attack. Rachel opens the door.

Rachel opens the door only a sliver.

DON DRAPER

I know it's late. I'm sorry.

RACHEL MENKEN

I got the telegram.

Don wedges his hand onto the doorframe. Rachel does not open the door any wider.

DON DRAPER

Let me in.

RACHEL MENKEN

Are you okay?

DON DRAPER

No.

Don Draper enters the apartment.

Don pushes the door open and goes right past Rachel to the center of the living room without waiting for her permission or for her to step aside. Rachel closes the door, but stays by it.

RACHEL MENKEN

You look terrible.

DON DRAPER

Can I get a drink?

RACHEL MENKEN

Of course.

Rachel moves to bar, starts to make a drink.

RACHEL MENKEN (CONT'D)

Are you happy with the doctors? I can have my father make a call.

DON DRAPER

I don't know, he's rich, they seem to be taking care of him.

RACHEL MENKEN

Is he okay? You can tell me, I'm not moving the account.

Rachel hands Don the drink.

Rachel gives Don the drink at arm's length. Rachel then takes a step back, maintaining a clear and ostensibly safe distance from Don.

DON DRAPER

He's gray and weak. His skin looks like paper.

RACHEL MENKEN

I'm sorry. He's your friend, isn't he?

DON DRAPER

What's the difference?

RACHEL MENKEN

You don't want to lose him.

Don moves in to kiss Rachel, Rachel backs away.

Rachel tightens her robe around her.

RACHEL MENKEN (CONT'D)

Don don't. What good is that gonna do? Feels like some solar eclipse, the end of the world, just do whatever you want?

DON DRAPER

I don't know.

RACHEL MENKEN

You do. You're exhausted. You just need sleep that's all.

Rachel crosses back to the door, intending to open it so Don will leave.

> DON DRAPER

I need to sit down.

Don moves to the couch.

> **Don sits in the middle of the couch.**
>
> DON DRAPER (CONT'D)

Sit with me.

> RACHEL MENKEN

Why?

> DON DRAPER

Cause I feel like you're looking right through me over there.

> RACHEL MENKEN

I'm not.

Rachel hesitates and moves to couch.

> **But Rachel does not sit.**
>
> DON DRAPER

I don't like feeling like this.

> RACHEL MENKEN

No one does.

> DON DRAPER

I remember the first time I was a pallbearer. I'd seen dead bodies before. I must've been 15, my aunt. I remember thinking, "They're letting me carry the box. They're letting me be this close to it. No one is hiding anything from me now." Then I looked over and saw all the old people, waiting together by the grave. And I remember thinking, "I just moved up a notch."

> **Rachel takes in this rare show of vulnerability from Don. She sits on the couch, but as far away from Don as possible.**
>
> RACHEL MENKEN

I've never heard you talk that much before. . .

                    DON DRAPER

Rachel.

                    RACHEL MENKEN

What do you want from me?

                    DON DRAPER

You know. I know you do, you know everything about me.

                    RACHEL MENKEN

I don't.

Don kisses Rachel.

> **Rachel lets the kiss go on for a couple of moments, then abruptly breaks it. She composes herself then stands, crosses only a couple of steps toward the door once again, intending to get Don to leave. Don rises from the couch and blocks her path to the door. Don reaches for her. Rachel takes a step backwards, avoiding his grasp.**

                    RACHEL MENKEN (CONT'D)

You don't want to do this. You have a wife, go to her.

                    DON DRAPER

Jesus Rachel. This is it. This is all there is, and I feel like it's slipping through my fingers like a handful of sand. This is it. This is all there is.

                    RACHEL MENKEN

That's just an excuse for bad behavior.

                    DON DRAPER

You don't really believe that.

> **Don takes Rachel by the hand and gently places her on the couch, on her back. He gets on top of her, between her legs.**

They lie down on the couch.

                    DON DRAPER (CONT'D)
I won't, unless you tell me you want this.

Rachel hesitates.

                    RACHEL MENKEN
Yes please.

Don undoes and opens Rachel's robe, revealing her nightie. Rachel closes her eyes. As Don pushes up her nightie and reaches for her panties we...

FADE TO BLACK.

Notes
1 Chan's amazingly inventive use of props could fill a book of its own.
2 To any actor, male or female, who is being pressured into doing something you never agreed to or wasn't in the script, all I can tell you is, *say no*, and walk away if you must. It's not worth it. But know what you're getting yourself into. If, for instance, you want to do a softcore erotic film, that's fine, just know that you'll probably be called upon to simulate graphic sex and be naked a lot. No judgment, just be sure you know the deal up front and don't kid yourself.

Works Cited
Body Heat. Directed by Lawrence Kasdan. Warner Bros., 1981.
Bridesmaids. Directed by Paul Feig. Universal Pictures, 2011.
Brokeback Mountain. Directed by Ang Lee. Focus Features, 2005.
Caine, Michael. *Acting in Film*. New York, Applause Books, 1990.
Calhoun, Zach. *People You Should Know. . . Leonora Pitts*. zackcalhoon.blogspot.com/, January 20, 2015.
Call Me By Your Name. Directed by Luca Guadagnino. Sony Pictures, 2017.
Dangerous Liaisons. Directed by Stephen Frears. Warner Bros., 1988.
Don't Look Now. Directed by Nicholas Roeg. Paramount Pictures, 1973.
Fast Times at Ridgemont High. Directed by Amy Heckerling. Universal Pictures, 1982.
L.A. Confidential. Directed by Curtis Hanson. Warner Bros., 1997.
Looking for Richard. Directed by Al Pacino. Fox Searchlight Pictures, 1996.
Mad Men. "Long Weekend," Season One, Episode 10. Created by Matthew Weiner. AMC Network, 2007. Television.
Monster's Ball. Directed by Marc Forster. Lion's Gate Films, 2001.
Munich. Directed by Steven Spielberg. Universal Pictures, 2005.
Team America: World Police. Directed by Matt Stone and Trey Parker. Paramount Pictures, 2005.
Wilde, Oscar. *The Plays of Oscar Wilde*. New York, Modern Library, 1980.
Y Tu Mamá También. Directed by Alfonso Cuarón. IFC Films, 2001.

9

ADJUSTMENTS AND RUN THROUGHS

Once again, the rehearsal process, if planned out logically, should naturally build upon itself. The good habits created in the actors in one set of rehearsals will support the next set. It's worth noting, in the interests of keeping your patience and sanity, that whenever a new element is added, it often seems that the work takes a step backward as the actors assimilate that new piece of the puzzle. Be cool. It will all come together. Keep pressing forward.

We previously noted that, at a certain point, big picture thematic discussions become counterproductive. (By the way, director-person: be aware of your own tendency to hold forth rather than actually rehearse. It likely means, just like the actors, you are either tired or afraid. That's okay. But be like Al Pacino. Jump in.) The same holds true for protracted symposiums on character analysis and interpretation once those choices have been made – not a good use of your time. You want the actors to trust their understanding of the story and the choices they made without constantly second-guessing themselves.

None if this is meant to suggest that things can't change – quite the opposite. If a bit of discussion is necessary to refocus or clarify a moment, have at it. Just remember, you don't want the rehearsal process to get stuck. We used to call it "paralysis by analysis." The *experience* of acting the scene will ultimately be the most powerful aspect of the rehearsal process for the actors.

As rehearsals progress, you will need to fine-tune and give the actors specific notes on certain moments. Refer to your key story points and, in the main, concentrate your direction there, but understand that at this point, once the foundation has been correctly laid, your directorial attention should be on the *details* of the scene. The notes you will give the actors fall into two basic categories: *creative* and *technical*. The creative notes, based on the actions being pursued in the scene, deal with the nuances of the actors' performances. The technical notes deal with the *presentation* of the scene.

Performance Notes: Adjustments

There are times when a moment might require a particular shading or nuance. Once again, it's your job as the director to communicate what you want the actor to do in clear, *actable* terms. In most cases, to get actors to adjust *how* they execute a particular moment, it is not necessary for them to completely change their actions. *Adverbs* are a useful tool to get the results you want from an actor at a particular moment. You remember adverbs from your fifth grade English lessons: those words that modify a verb. According to our friends at Merriam-Webster's Dictionary, most adverbs are formed by adding "ly" to an adjective: bold/boldly, solid/solidly, heavy/heavily, etc. There are other types of adverbs and adverbial clauses, but we'll stick with the "ly" for now words because they are the easiest to work with, and you can always contact your fifth grade teacher if you feel that you require a further grammatical breakdown. I'm sure they'll be thrilled to hear from you.

In terms of acting and directing, adverbs fall into three buckets:

1. *Purely physical adjustments.* Adverbs such as quickly, slowly, quietly, loudly, etc. are clear, easy to process, and easy to execute. A simple physical adjustment is often all an actor needs to provide the necessary behavior or the illusion thereof. But sometimes these types of adjustments can feel incomplete or inorganic to an actor. A change in a person's physical dynamics is a product of an internal response to some form of stimulus, either external or internal. Why, for instance, might a person choose to speak more slowly? There are many reasons: they are not being understood, the other

person is thick-headed, they are savoring a moment, they're tired, they want to create suspense in the listener, etc. Or, in terms of externals, a slower speech rhythm might be a function of the character's dialect, upbringing, cognitive abilities, or social class. Sometimes a physical adjustment without some form of attendant intentionality does not work for the actor. Sometimes it does.

2. *Purely emotional adjustments.* Adverbs like happily, angrily, fearfully, etc. are not your keenest move. They are static emotional states, and it's much harder to incorporate them into a dynamic, outwardly directed action. What tends to happen is that actors will substitute the adjustment for the action, so they end up playing happiness, anger, fear, etc. and the action goes out the window. Emotionally based directing leads to self-conscious, emotionally based acting (indicating), and that, as we know, is the quickest pathway to the dark side.

3. *Temperamental adjustments.* Adverbs in this category ask for an attitudinal adjustment that may tilt the actor in a certain emotional direction, but they are *playable* in that they can be easily incorporated into an action. Adverbs such as reasonably, carefully, forcefully, patiently, bitterly, boldly, etc. fall into this bucket and are the most useful.

But wait, there's more. . .

Another useful set of directorial tools is, wait for it, *verbs*. For instance, lecture, dismiss, bully, reason, confront, praise, apologize, bulldoze, chastise, instruct, ridicule – any active verb that can be immediately acted upon at a particular moment as a function of the main scene action is generally effective. Also, little "mini actions" – quick, active phrases – are also effective. "Read him the riot act!" "Stand up to her!" "Call his bluff." "Draw the line." "Get him to listen."

We could go on forever with verbs and verb clauses, but you get the idea. The upshot is, the endgame of any piece of direction must result in a *playable* moment. What all of these tools have in common is that they are action-oriented. The rest is just semantics, so use whatever verbiage you're comfortable with – the grammar police are not watching, and if you get really stuck, once again, call your fifth grade teacher.[1]

Pauses

Some actors love pauses; they'll camp on a pause for a complete lunar cycle if given the chance. Other actors don't like to pause because they feel self-conscious and unsure of what to do. Also, you know, actors tend to like to talk, so many of them want to get back to the dialogue ASAP. But an investigation of why a character chooses to stay silent, even if only for a moment, inevitably leads to a deeper understanding of that moment and how it serves the scene. As the director, your job is to help the actors discover what is really going on in those silences.

Effective pauses create tension and cause the audience to wonder what will happen next. Also, great writers such as Harold Pinter use pauses to create the *rhythm* of the scene. They are as important as the actual dialogue! So when rehearsing, encourage the actors to lean into the pauses. Let them take their time; you can tighten up pauses that go on too long in subsequent rehearsals. But consider how *not* speaking affects the actors in terms of the pursuit of their actions. From the outset, you as the director must be clear on how the pauses advance the narrative in the scene and make all choices accordingly. Eventually, in terms of staging, decide if you want physical activity or stillness.

A comedic example of the effective use of the pause is Larry David in *Curb Your Enthusiasm*. One of Larry's signature bits is "the stare-down" – an exaggerated, extended examination of someone's facial expression when he thinks that person is lying. Larry gets almost nose to nose and tilts his head at various angles, probing for something that will tip him off or get the other person to break down and admit the truth. The bit always ends with him deciding whether or not the other person is on the level; on occasion the test fails completely and he's no more sure of the truth than when he began. Sometimes the stare-down goes on for a very long time as Larry doggedly tries to expose his stoic or perplexed opponent; prolonging the bit not only increases the tension in the scene but is also very funny in its absurdity. (My personal favorite is when Jerry Seinfeld turns the tables and stares down Larry, who freezes in fear like a deer in the headlights.)

Using Larry's example, we can break a pause down into three parts: *the moment before* the pause that precipitates the need to stop speaking; *the pause itself*; and the *outcome* of the pause. The latter is a simple but effective trick that advances the story: make sure that the actor(s) has a *new moment* coming out of the pause from where they started whenever possible.

Another lovely example of an actor crushing it in a pause is Charles Durning in the film *Tootsie*. (Warning: spoilers ahead.) The penultimate scene in the film takes place in a bar in upstate New York. A few weeks after Michael Dorsey (Dustin Hoffman) – an actor who had gained national celebrity by pretending to be an female actress appearing on a soap opera – revealed his true identity as a man on live television, he sits down next to Les (Durning), a widower who had fallen in love with Dorothy, Michael's female alter ego. Les gives Michael, whom he does not recognize at first, a friendly nod as he watches a prize fight on the television behind the bar. A moment later, it dawns on Les who Michael is, but he continues to stare coldly at the television. Then, Les gives Michael a look of contained rage and turns away again, pretending to watch the fight, his facial expression betraying his humiliation, anger, and pain. Still, no words. Michael then puts the engagement ring box Les had given "Dorothy" on the bar. Les shoves it back and mutters, "Outside. Give it to me outside." Another silence before Les finally forces himself to face Michael and ask, "Why'd you do it?" It's a great piece of acting from Mr. Durning and an object lesson in the power of silence when the actor is truly connected to the moment. His array of emotions, facial expressions, and body language tell the story as profoundly as any line of dialogue ever could. *Capisce?*

Initially, actors don't have to know why they are pausing. Simply placing them into that potentially awkward moment, even before you stage it or give them any direction, is often enough for them to discover the deeper content of those moments of silence. At the very least, it will prime them for your direction.

So, in theory, you've now done all your creative directing: character analysis, blocking, etc. There's not much more to say in terms of what you want from your actors as you begin run throughs of the play. What now?

Run Throughs: Technical Notes

At this point in the rehearsal process, the emphasis shifts once again. As the director, your efforts should now be oriented toward the *presentation* of the scene, so once again you'll have to focus, by proxy, on the audience's experience. This is not to say that you can't continue to give performance notes, but keep them clear and simple. Also, believe it or not, complicated or overly analytical acting notes can be very counterproductive at this point. The actors know what is required of them, and their performances will begin to truly blossom with repetitive practice, that is, running the scenes over and over. Repetition is not only the mother of skill but the mother of good *unconscious* habits. Sometimes the best piece of direction you can give is, after showering your actors with love, affection, and praise worthy of the gods, "Run it again."

When I was a wee lad in drama school, a teacher gave what sounded at the time like a really goofy piece of direction, but one that has stayed with me for decades. The specifics have long since faded from memory, but he said to one of my classmates, "Do exactly what you're doing, just do it more." My teacher was not advocating for the actor to push or fake it or get hammy; his point was that the actor had made all the right choices and was doing the right thing in the scene, and he wanted the actor to trust their instincts and *commit fully*. Nothing more needed to be said. Believe me, you'll find yourself at this point again and again; there's no need to fix what isn't broken, just get your actors to lean in hard on their actions and trust their moment-to-moment instincts. So okay, I hear you ask, *then what should I focus on?* The answer is *stagecraft*.

Every scene must be crafted so that its presentation is clear and fun to watch. This is where stagecraft comes into play. In particular, as a director, you will always need time to recalibrate when you move from the rehearsal room to the actual performance space for run throughs. Even though you have been – hopefully – rehearsing using the dimensions of the performance space, you will find that the timing of things like crosses and business might need to change once you are working in the actual theatre. Don't worry if a few moments get temporarily lost; once the actors acclimate to the space, they'll pull it together.

It's helpful, when first working in the performance space, to do a "stumble through" – a stop and start rehearsal – wherein you work through any moments that need adjusting. Then, run the scenes without stopping so the actors can get the flow. You want to correct any technical issues (other than stuff you'll deal with in tech rehearsals) right away so you can begin proper run throughs. If a scene is still problematic in run throughs, schedule a separate rehearsal to tighten it up.

Here's a list of what you need to be aware of so every scene plays clean and tight.

1. *Pace.* There's an old joke about directors: at the end of the day, they only have three arrows in their quiver: faster, funnier, and louder. But here's the deal: rarely has an audience ever complained about a scene going too fast. So, at this point you have to suck the dead air out of every scene. The oldest trick in the book is for actors to pick up their cues; cut down the amount of space *between* the lines, and then the actors don't have to rush when speaking. But if the scene gets too slow, the audience gets bored and the moments where you have crafted a pause will lose their dramatic weight. Also, remember that pace is not just about going fast. Pace is also a function of *dynamics*, so when there's a need to pause or slow things down, make sure the actors adhere to the timing you want.

    One of your primary responsibilities in crafting the presentation of a scene is *time management.* Time onstage is compressed; for theatrical stories to be well-told and hold the audience's attention, every moment must count in terms of the narrative. An excellent tool to tighten the pace is the *speed through.* Have the actors run their lines as fast as they can, while still being clearly understood. Emphasize picking up the cues. This is not an acting rehearsal; it's a technical exercise to habitualize quickening the pace.

2. *Staging.* Make sure the sight lines are as open to the audience as possible. Remind the actors to cheat out whenever necessary. Also, review all stage business to make sure it's being executed smoothly. If anything seems unintentionally awkward, stop and fix it. Now you can't rewrite the script, so much of this obviously falls on the writer, but in terms of staging, ask yourself if everything you are seeing and hearing is furthering the narrative. If it isn't, fix it or cut it.

3. *Pauses.* A pause that you allowed to go on indefinitely in rehearsal so the actors could discover the nature of the moment might now

be dragging down the pace of the scene, so tighten it up so the scene keeps moving.
    4. *Vocal levels*. In the theatre, if actors are not speaking up, their acting sucks. End of story. You will often find that the vocal levels at first feel inadequate when run throughs begin in the actual performance space, so remind the actors to speak up right away.

Final Thoughts

As the director, you must understand, and make peace with the fact, that you are ultimately going to turn the play over to the actors. While staying true to your direction and the requirements of the text, they are the ones who are going to tell the story. By this time, the actors own it, for better or worse.

This is not to suggest that you can't continue to give notes and fine-tune, either creatively or technically, right up to opening night. You will see things in dress rehearsals and previews that were not clear or in evidence in rehearsal, especially in comedy. The addition of a live audience – the final piece of the rehearsal puzzle – is a crucial step that will change the performances, usually for the better. You may give a ton of notes in the week or two before you open – that's great, it's your job to hone in on the details. But the time is coming for you to shut the fuck up.

Yes, you read that right. *Shut the fuck up.*

Resist the urge to make major changes or otherwise turn things upside down in the homestretch of rehearsals. I don't mean to play amateur shrink here – okay, you got me, I kind of do – but that impulse to change what was working just fine is your own insecurity making itself felt. I'm eminently unqualified to help you out on a psychological level, other than to offer a piece of advice I learned as a writer. My writing partner and I know that a scene is done when the changes don't make it any better, just different. If futzing with a scene results in purely lateral changes, be content that you've done your best and move on. Don't obsess. Don't micromanage. It's too late for that anyway.

It's also worth noting, especially in an extended rehearsal process, that things can begin to feel stale; the funny line or bit no longer elicits laughter because everyone has seen it over and over. An affecting moment might feel static or flat for the same reason, but trust that when you put those moments in front of an audience, they will come back to life. (Be aware of actors starting to push or overact at this point, and be sure to put out those fires as they occur.)

Your notes on the final few rehearsals should be lean and mean because you do not want to overburden the actors by forcing them to process a lot of new information. You want to reinforce the good habits that they have created throughout the rehearsal process and give them the freedom to play. The endgame of all your preparation, all your direction, and all the notes you give is that the actors *assimilate it and forget about it*. Get out of the actors' heads. Only then does the alchemical magic that is great acting have a chance to manifest.

You've done your job. Congrats. Go have a beer.

Director's Final Checklist

1. Are the actors speaking up and speaking clearly?
2. Are the actors clearly visible to the audience?
3. Are actors picking up their cues and respecting the pauses?
4. Are the actors committing to their actions? (If not, gently remind them to do so.)
5. Is all stage business and physical choreography playing cleanly?
6. Are the sight lines working?

Note

1 Pick up a copy of *Actions: The Actors' Thesaurus* by Marina Calderone and Maggie Lloyd-Williams. It's super useful in terms of helping actors and directors expand their vocabulary. However, I would not subscribe to their theories on acting and script analysis.

Works Cited

Curb Your Enthusiasm. Created by Larry David. HBO, 2000.
Tootsie. Directed by Sydney Pollack. Columbia Pictures, 1982.

10

COMEDY

THE SERIOUS BUSINESS OF HUMOR

> Comedy is the imitation of an inferior man.
>
> *Aristotle*

So you might be wondering, why a separate chapter on comedy? Because if you want to direct comedy, you need to understand the mechanics of the genre. It's also easy, as a director and a performer, to be led astray in the pursuit of laughs because, let's be honest, getting a huge laugh onstage is the most fun you can have with your clothes on. It's very addictive and, thus, fraught with temptation for the actor to abdicate the fundamentals of good acting. Comedy, although similar to drama in many ways, plays by its own set of rules that are essential not only to acting and directing but writing as well. At the end of the chapter, we'll look at how to apply Practical Aesthetics and some of the other directing principles to comedy.

In his book *Jokes and Their Relation to the Unconscious*, noted stand-up comic Sigmund Freud ("Oedipus, his mom, and dad walk into a bar . . .") dissects the nature of the joke and its social function. He writes, "We have already learned from the connection of jokes with caricature that they must bring something forward which is concealed or hidden."

Using Freudian terminology, the controlling superego allows the ego to generate humor as a form of psychological relief. We laugh at political folly because it helps eradicate, or at least live with, the fear that our leaders are incompetent, evil, or nuts. (Or all three.) So comedy, like the joke itself, creates the emotional buffer that allows the audience to deal with aspects of life that they might otherwise find too unsettling to consciously confront. Laughter provides a release of repressed anxiety or the gratification of a repressed desire. Great comedy often takes on the angst of modern life: our institutions are crumbling around us, relationships are all doomed, and human nature is, at its core, venal, amoral, and cruel. People. We're a laugh a minute, ain't we? Yes, the audience comes to have a good time, but knowingly or not, they also come to watch comedy do what it does best: demolish hypocrisy and roast sanctimonious sacred cows.

Farce: The Mother of All Comedy Styles

In this chapter, we will examine the rules of farce, which date back to the dawn of theatre, maybe the dawn of time. Farce is arguably the most influential and pervasive comedic form because it isn't just a style, it's also a *vocabulary* that contains all of the nucleic elements of comedy, which can be selectively retrofitted to other comedic styles (see the appendix at the end of this chapter). As a director, you'll be able to employ these ideas in terms of character choices and staging in a manner consistent with the style and tone of the material. Not all comedy is farce, but there are, at the very least, trace elements of farce in all other forms of comedy.

Farce is defined as "a comedy characterized by broad satire and improbable situations." It aims to entertain the audience through circumstances that are highly exaggerated, extravagant, and thus improbable. It is also characterized by physical humor, the deliberate use of absurdity or nonsense, and broadly stylized performances. Setting is also important in farce, as the protagonist is often at odds with their physical environment. In farce, the central character often does not belong in the story's setting which makes it that much more difficult for them to function. (In Hollywood, this is known as the "fish out of water" story.[1])

Farce by its nature is not naturalistic. In fact, most forms of comedy are not meant to strictly document reality – they mean to *explicate* it through exaggeration. So farce, at its best, functions *in extremis*. Indeed, human folly, in all its maddeningly repetitive glory, is the sweet spot for all great comedy. What is demanded of the farceur or satirist is to crank up the character's flaws – and the resultant behavior – far beyond that which would be acceptable in drama. But, for a comedic story to work, it must still be grounded in some fundamental human truth. For instance, *Blazing Saddles*, Mel Brooks's classic film farce about a Black sheriff in the Old West, in addition to being a fish out of water story, is at heart an indictment of racism.

Great comedy results from choosing rich targets. The satirist goes after what's wrong with society, so comedy exaggerates the foibles of human nature in order to have larger, juicier marks at which to take aim. Thus, we find that farce is largely about the *deflation* of characters who are selfish, pompous, vain, egotistical, dishonest, greedy, etc. There is rarely complex character development in farce; the characters' needs are straightforward and easily understood by the audience, so profound change and growth are not necessary in order for the audience to have a satisfying experience. In fact, the audience will put up with a lot more shenanigans in a farce than in a drama. The difference lies in the *duration* and *degree* of socially unacceptable behavior.

In a drama, if the duration of the hero's antisocial behavior goes on for too long, the audience's empathy will dissipate, and they will be disinclined to root for them. The audience will check out because they've stopped caring. *The Sopranos*, as brilliant as that show was, suffered from this problem in its last couple of seasons. For years, the writers dangled a thread of hope, however faint, that mob boss Tony Soprano might turn the corner and become a decent person. His wife Carmela lived in that delusion for her entire adult life, but after a while, the audience knew that it was never going to happen, so they basically gave up on Tony. By contrast, it's perfectly fine to have asshole heroes in comedy as long as, 1. they get their comeuppance and 2. they are funny.

Degree is the other barometer that sets the off the emotional trip wire in the audience. For the dramatic hero or antihero, if the "crimes" are too dear, the audience withdraws their empathy and only wants the character to be punished.[2] For instance, there was a spate of martial arts films in the late 1980s and early 1990s that featured a protagonist who was so brutal and so relished sickening violence that he was in fact more psychotic and dangerous than the bad guys he was pursuing. The theatrical spectacle of violence aside, many audience members found it hard to root for a hero who tortured people simply for the joy of making them suffer. The painfully clichéd trope of those stories – "I need information from this dirtbag in order to save the blah blah blah" – ultimately did little to change the audience's contempt for the hero.

Further, in drama there comes a point where the audience, when confronted with too much cruelty, simply checks out because they can only take so much in terms of realistic depictions of actual human suffering. In the thriller *The Killer Inside Me*, Casey Affleck beats poor Jessica Alba to death so brutally that by the end of the "fight" Alba's face is a bloody, unrecognizable mass of pulp. Whatever dramatic point the scene tried to make was lost in its hyperrealistic depiction of violence, and many audience members reported being so unsettled that they either stopped caring or stopped watching the film altogether. (Of course, there is an audience for this sort of thing, but the psychology of the "torture porn" audience is way over my pay grade and, you know, not funny.)

Farce, on the other hand, allots more time for the hero – and everyone else – to behave badly, and on a much grander scale. Indeed, many comedies actually turn on the hero being rather despicable, the comic equivalent of the dramatic antihero. *Bad Santa* is an excellent example – as written by Glenn Ficarra and John Requa and uncompromisingly played by Billy Bob Thornton. Willie (Thornton), the world's worst department store Santa, is an unapologetic, misanthropic douchebag whose turnaround comes late in the story. But it works because the hard-drinking Willie is aptly punished for his bad behavior, and all the terrible stuff he does is really, really funny. (The scene where Willie comes to work hung over and then proceeds to trash Santaland, to the horror of the assembled parents and children, is one of the film's many dark comic gems.)

In cinema, we find the equivalent of the indestructible, comedic protagonist in the action-adventure hero: James Bond or Indiana Jones must be superhuman for the audience to enjoy watching them get the hell knocked out of them. But naturalistic drama in film often finds itself walking a narrow tightrope of credibility: if the characters survive violence that is too brutal, the audience doesn't buy it, but if the drama is too realistic, we're back to the problem of audience alienation found in *The Killer Inside Me*. Comedy, by its very nature and the rules discussed herein, is free from these polarizing constraints. Directors must recognize that comedy often turns on extremes and make choices regarding the actors that take things as far as the material will support.

The Comedic Premises (Premesi?)

From a writing perspective, there are two basic ways to approach the comedic premise: create a situation that is absurd to begin with or take a serious situation and treat it comically.

The *inherently absurd premise* takes improbable protagonists, surrounds them with improbable supporting characters, and places them all in an improbable situation. The audience accepts even the most bizarre and impossible circumstances, because they understand that comedy needn't be realistic, just funny. The writing here turns largely on *absurd juxtapositions*: putting elements together that do not ordinarily coexist. One finds many great examples of this approach in short-form comedy, particularly the better television sketch shows.

The original *Monty Python's Flying Circus* BBC TV program, oh wait, I'm sorry, they're British, so TV *programme*, is a Holy Bible of these comedic conceits that largely turn on juxtaposing unlikely elements together for comedic effect. For instance:

The Ministry of Silly Walks. In a satire of stodgy government agencies, John Cleese, all elbows, knees, and impossibly long legs flailing about, plays the minister of a British government bureau in charge of handing out grants for people to develop silly walks. He takes his position dead seriously, as does Michael Palin, who timidly tries to win a grant. The sketch is full of over-the-top, deftly executed physical comedy, but the humor lies in the *juxtaposition*. There's nothing particularly funny about a government ministry or silly walks without context. Putting these two elements together creates the comedic effect. In sketches like this, it's incumbent on the director to make sure the staging and gags are precise and that the actors respect the rules of the sketch by completely accepting the premise.

Homie the Clown. A recurring character on the 1990s sketch show *In Living Color*, Damon Wayans' Homie was a clown-for-hire who worked children's birthday parties. Homie was, however, a bitter, angry, chain-smoking fellow who used each gig as an excuse to rant about the unfairness of life and the many indignities he felt he was forced to suffer. He actually hated kids and cared little about entertaining them. The juxtaposition here is a person whose temperament and personality are spectacularly ill-suited to his job. The director's primary responsibility is to highlight the character's bitterness, which is as discomfiting as it is funny.

Now let's look at the *serious premise treated comedically*. In *The Life of the Drama*, Professor Eric Bentley's lively, practitioner-oriented book on theatrical styles, the author observes that any great comedy should have the underpinnings of a great drama. Take away the funny lines and physical bits, and the bones of the story should hold up dramatically. *Blazing Saddles* is a great example of this principle at work. Preston Sturges' classic comedy *The Lady Eve*, the story of a heartless con woman settling the score against the mark who dumped her and who then discovers that she's really in love with him, could very easily play as a dark noir drama. Similarly, Stanley Kubrick's Cold War satire *Dr. Strangelove* also works as a tense vérité thriller about an impending nuclear war.[3]

For writers, the bar is raised much higher when treating a serious subject with comedic intent because it's far more difficult to create true emotional and intellectual resonance without sanctimony in a comedy. Neil Simon essentially said that he became a better writer by embracing serious subject matter in a comic way. But, as we will discuss, either approach to comedy needs an underlying seriousness in order to work, and that adherence to truth within the improbable nature of farce is one of the director's primary responsibilities, particularly with regard to the actors' performances.

The Principles of Farce

What follows are the core principles we will be working with, all of which resonate across the main theatrical disciplines: acting, directing, and writing. But every trope we discuss is essential for the comedy director and can be selectively employed at every stage of the rehearsal process, from the first table read, to staging, to final run throughs.

Play It Straight

The first and most unassailable principle of comedy is to take it seriously; in other words, *play it straight*. Comedy is always based on truth. Laughter, as much as it's an expression of delight and a release of anxiety, is also a sign of *recognition*. We laugh, collectively, because we recognize a common truth that is relevant to our lives. So, actors need to find the truth of their characters first, and then the humor will follow.

> Even in the wildest farce, the characters take their circumstances seriously, and so must the actors.

The hallmark of great comedic actors is the ability to be totally believable as well as funny. In fact, the crazier the circumstances get, the more seriously the actors must take them or the audience will not be emotionally involved and, thus, will not care what happens to the characters. It will also cheapen the humor.

The great Mel Brooks described it best in a *Playboy* interview:

> There's one thing you've got to understand before you can direct comedy. Comedy is serious – deadly serious. Never, never try to be funny! The actors must be serious. Only the situation must be absurd. Funny is in the writing, not in the performing. If the situation isn't absurd, no amount of hoke will help. And another thing, the more serious the situation, the funnier the comedy can be. The greatest comedy plays against the greatest tragedy. Comedy is a red-rubber ball and if you throw it against a soft, funny wall, it will not come back. But if you throw it against the hard wall of ultimate reality, it will bounce back and be very lively, Vershteh, goy bastard? No offense. Very, very few people understand this.

The single greatest lesson that all great comic actors, from Lucille Ball to Jerry Lewis to Joanna Lumley to Jim Carrey, understand is this: *whatever is happening to the characters may be funny to us, but it's not funny to them*. Great comedic actors know that the more absurd the situation, the more devoted to the truth they must be.

If the actors start telegraphing to the audience that they're not taking the script seriously or mug to get a laugh at the expense of the story, it's a pyrrhic victory: the laugh is not worth it if it damages the credibility of the character and the narrative. I've always taken things as far as I could when directing comedy, but what William Faulkner said certainly applies: "In writing, you must kill all your darlings." I've laid to rest many funny moments because they were not appropriate or were extraneous to the scene, and yes, my better angels told me I did the right thing, but the laugh whore inside me still thinks I'm a moron. (By the way, my one-man show, *The Laugh Whore Inside Me*, will be coming soon to a theatre near. . . someone.)

One of the best and most ubiquitous examples of actors playing it straight is the entire cast of the American version of *The Office*. The characters take their needs and desires seriously, and the audience will never catch the actors disrespecting their circumstances. Dwight Schrute, brilliantly played by Rainn Wilson, is the king of taking things seriously, no matter how absurd. Dwight is also driven by two very clear ambitions that permeate everything he does: to move up in the company and to win the approval of his boss, Michael Scott (wonderfully played by Steve Carell.) It's particularly hilarious when Dwight's two objectives come into conflict with each other. It's also worth noting that even when Michael tries to be funny, there's an underlying emotional need: he is desperate to be loved and accepted. The show's humor, which sometimes veers into decidedly uncomfortable waters, is buttressed by the fact the Michael's frequent attempts at humor usually fail miserably.[4]

The Indestructible Hero

Farce is largely anchored by the notion that no matter what occurs, no matter what physical and/or emotional torture the heroes are subjected to, they will *survive* and, certainly according to the rules of classic theatrical farce, get what they want in the end. Traditionally, the audience must empathize with and root for the protagonist, but never truly fear for the character's life. That would spoil the fun and force the level of physical and emotional punishment inflicted on the hero to conform to the laws of realism, which is a comedic buzzkill. In farce, the characters must have the holy hell kicked out of them physically, spiritually, emotionally, or any other way you can imagine. But the audience needs to know that the hero(es) will survive, so farce provides the audience with a de facto safety net that allows it to laugh at violence, bad behavior, and just about all forms of human suffering. For this reason, characters in farce are often superhuman and can withstand copious amounts of abuse and come back for more.

The Monty Python guys figured out a paradigm that helps to create this reassurance for the audience: as long as the person on the receiving end of the violence or mistreatment doesn't mind too much, it's okay, even up to and including death. For instance, take King Arthur's sword fight with the Black Knight in *Monty Python and the Holy Grail*. Arthur literally hacks his adversary's limbs off one by one. But the Black Knight sees each severed limb as a minor setback, and refuses to admit defeat. To wit: upon losing an arm, he glances at the blood spurting from his shoulder, says "Tis but a scratch," and resumes the fight. Left a limbless stump on the ground, the Black Knight, *still* refusing to admit defeat says, "We'll call it a draw." This comically incongruous reframing of the fight gives the audience permission to laugh. Yeah, the Black Knight lost his arms and legs, but he'll get over it.

To fully understand the concept of indestructibility, we need look no further than Warner Bros. cartoons. Here's some of the agony and torture our favorite WB cartoon characters have been subjected to:

- Daffy Duck gets burned to a mound of ash, with the exception of his beak.
- Wile E. Coyote rams into the side of a mountain, or crashes through a billboard, or falls off a cliff into the bottom of the Grand Canyon due to faulty rocket skates (damn you, Acme Company!).
- Yosemite Sam gets blown up by playing a certain note on a piano.
- Marvin the Martian gets blown up by his space modulator.
- Bugs Bunny shoots a guy who can't stop coughing as he tries to start his piano concert.
- Elmer Fudd blows Daffy's head off over and over and over and over (poor Daffy, the abuse he endures could fill an encyclopedia).

Now, for those of you old enough to have actually seen a WB cartoon, here's a pop quiz: after the violence, how are the characters in the next scene? That's right! They're just fine. (Well, Wile E. Coyote might have a cast or a sling or a bandage or two, but hey, he just fell off a cliff, so we'll call that a win.) It's not that the violence doesn't hurt, but characters in farce are, as a rule, more resilient than their dramatic counterparts and, thus, do not suffer realistic consequences.

Here are a few more examples of exaggerated violence in farce:

- *Return of the Pink Panther*: The epic Clouseau/Kato opening fight in which the two characters trash the house in a fight seemingly to the death.

- *Saturday Night Live*: Dan Ackroyd, as Julia Child, "The French Chef," accidentally chops off his hand but keeps going with the recipe as blood spurts everywhere.
- *There's Something About Mary*: Ben Stiller gets his dick caught in his zipper before the senior prom.
- *The 40-Year-Old Virgin*: The hair removal scene ("Kelly Clarkson!")
- *The Nice Guys*: Russell Crowe beats the shit out of Ryan Gosling
- *Dodgeball*: The wrench-throwing training scene. ("You can dodge a wrench, you can dodge a ball.")

The same paradigm regarding physical violence holds true for *emotional* violence; referring back to the Pythons, if the person on the receiving end can handle it, then the audience can find it funny.

A great example of gleeful emotional violence is the film *In the Loop*. Based on the hit BBC sitcom *The Thick of It*, *In the Loop* is a political satire about a group of American and British political and military operatives attempting to prevent a war over a British politician's slip of the tongue. The lacerating insults and invective from Scottish spin doctor Malcolm Tucker (Peter Capaldi) achieve a kind of soaring, scatological poetry as he lays waste to the self-esteem of anyone who gets in his way or otherwise annoys him. For example:

> Your *purview*? Where do you think you are, some regency costume drama? This is a government department, not a fucking Jane fucking Austen novel! Allow me to pop a jaunty little bonnet on your purview and ram it up your shitter with a lubricated horse-cock!

And:

> You breathe a word of this to anyone, you mincing fucking cunt, and I will tear your fucking skin off, I will wear it to your mother's birthday party and I will rub your nuts up and down her leg whilst whistling Bohemian fucking Rhapsody, right?

And yet, those on the receiving end manage to survive; even supporting characters in a farce must be resilient.

Farce also traffics in human suffering and the grotesque. Python's rules regarding violence also apply here – as long as the "victim" doesn't mind, bring it on. It's even better if the character transforms their disability into an asset. Quasimodo, the titular character in *The Hunchback of Notre Dame*, is a tragic figure; Marty Feldman's Igor (pronounced "Eye-gor") in *Young Frankenstein* is not only unbothered by his physical deformity but uses it to confuse and confound Dr. Frankenstein and various others whenever the mood strikes him.

Base Appetites and Shamelessness

Characters in farce are often extremely selfish and are driven by base human appetites such as greed, lust, power, revenge, gluttony, envy, and vanity – the whole pupu platter of deadly sins and then some. Targets, right? So, the stakes in farce must be high both in the writing and in the actors' performances; good comic actors know that they must pursue their intentions with complete, often maniacal commitment, no matter how trivial the characters' desires might seem to the audience.

Characters in farce are also shameless in the pursuit of their desires; no matter how base, low, or dishonest, they feel *entitled* to get what they want and will go to extreme lengths to get it. Shamelessness is essential to the construction of character and story in farce. Shamelessness also works in the opposite direction: characters in farce might have huge, worldly ambitions, and once again they'll stop at nothing to get what they want. (Dr. Evil, anyone?)

Shamelessness is also crucial in satire because it opens the door to anarchy. The humor of the Marx Brothers, still cinema's greatest comic anarchists, largely turns on this principle. Wherever the brothers showed up, the prevailing order, be it a hotel (*The Cocoanuts*), a rich woman's estate (*Animal Crackers*), a college (*Horse Feathers*), or an entire nation on the brink of war (*Duck Soup*), was sure to fall apart. And because the boys, like my personal hero Bugs Bunny, could get away with murder, the audience members, as Freud suggests, were free to enjoy and indulge their own anti-authoritarian impulses.

Directors need to remember that the actors in farce must commit with abandon to their actions. Actors must not judge, nor do they need to justify the characters' desires; they simply need to *embrace* them.

Big Things Made Small, Small Things Made Big

Comedy largely turns on a *skewed perspective*, in which a character's worldview is often out of adjustment to what most people might consider normal (whatever that is). This reversal of expectations can, somewhat simplistically, be described as "big things made small, small things made big."

"Big things made small" creates a point of view that lowers the significance of an event in the eyes of the character. It's funny because of the absurdity of this perspective. In fact, in the heightened reality of comedy, the absurd is largely normalized. A great example of this comedic point of view is Bill Murray's entire performance in *Ghostbusters*. No matter how frightening or outrageous his encounters with the paranormal, Dr. Venkman never loses his composure and even treats getting "slimed" by a semicorporeal ghost as just part of the job, just another day in the life of a ghostbuster.

Another example is Kimmy Schmidt's eternal optimism in the sitcom *Unbreakable Kimmy Schmidt*. Kimmy (the wonderful Ellie Kemper) was a prisoner in an underground bunker for 15 years, essentially a sex slave for a would-be cult leader, yet she treats that experience – which certainly has the makings of an intense, probing, super-depressing psychological drama – as just a bit of bad luck. Her eternal optimism minimizes the trauma and allows the audience to laugh, even at the flashback scenes set in the bunker with the other two female prisoners. Kimmy is a survivor; that's why we can laugh.

In actor-speak, this particular reversal of values is also known as "underplaying." However, an underplayed response or point of view is not simply a function of a lower speaking volume and/or a lack of emotional intensity – it can actually take place at the top of an actor's lungs. For example, although, strictly speaking, not a farce, the scene in *Pulp Fiction* where Vince (John Travolta) mistakenly shoots young Marvin (Phil LaMarr) in the face, splattering his blood all over the car, is a great example of this principle. Vince's partner Jules (Samuel L. Jackson), now covered in Marvin's blood and guts, is not upset that a nice, blameless kid was killed, he's super-annoyed that he and his car are a mess and thus they have to find a place to hide out. Travolta plays off of Jackson perfectly, taking an aggrieved stance in the scene by insisting that Jules is overreacting to an innocent mistake. All the while, what's left of poor Marvin is sprawled in the backseat. It's horrifying but also very funny because of Vince and Jules' skewed perspective. (Travolta's underplayed delivery of the line "Oh man, I shot Marvin in the face" is pure comic perfection.)

The skewed perspective inherent in "small things made big" is equally as effective. Characters in comedy will often obsess on things that most of us could either do without or burn a limited number of calories to achieve. But once again, it must be of paramount importance to the character, because only then can the comedy be taken to the extreme. For example, in *National Lampoon's Vacation*, Clark Griswold (Chevy Chase) has a very simple intention: to take his family on a vacation to Wally World, a Disneyland-esque amusement park. (Warning: spoilers ahead.) But each obstacle on the cross-country drive eats away, little by little, at Clark's sanity, so when he finally arrives at Wally World only to discover the park is closed for repairs, he loses it and forces a hapless security guard (the great John Candy) at gunpoint to take his now-horrified family on the rides. It's very funny, but also unsettling; if you can pull off that one-two punch as a writer, you'll probably be able to buy a house in Malibu.

"Small things made big" is also an excellent tool with which to satirize pretty much anything that speaks to petty, selfish, or boorish behavior or, the great mass murderer of comedy, political correctness. Key and Peele's sketch "Overly Offended Co-workers" finds a gay man, a woman, and a black man in their boss's office. The boss has asked them to listen to his speech for the upcoming company picnic to make sure there is nothing offensive. The rolling joke of the sketch is that the trio is so full of outrage over *everything* that and they interpret even the most innocent remark from the boss as an assault on the group that they each represent. Even a simple request to raise a hand if they find anything objectionable is met with an absurd and completely unwarranted level of hostility.

In addition to shameless desires, what also comes into play here in "small things made big" is the *well-intended*. Departing somewhat from the base and shameless, in farce even a well-intended desire can provoke extreme behavior. In *Serial Mom*, John Waters' farce/satire of middle America, Mom (Kathleen Turner) wants nothing more than the ideal suburban life for her family and community. She is driven by her relentless desire for the perfect, orderly life and will lethally dispatch anyone who violates her sense of propriety, including a neighbor with lazy recycling habits. Mom even goes after a woman who dares to wear white after Labor Day because it so offends her sensibilities. (And let's be honest – that's just wrong.)

Rising Complications and the Unexpected

Farce is full of many convenient, outrageous, perfectly ill-timed coincidences and a ton of "oh shit" moments that the audience not only forgives but demands. In fact, the more the merrier. So, it is incumbent on the actor to respond accordingly to the many twists and turns of a well-constructed farce. Characters in farce live in a world of sudden surprises that complicate the plot and provide unexpected obstacles, so the actors must fully acknowledge these moments *as they occur* and decide, in analytical terms, whether to change tactics or change actions. From a director's perspective, these moments are often key story points and will figure prominently not only in the actors' choices but also the staging of each scene.

Great farces are devised with exacting precision both in dialogue and physical action. In a typical bedroom farce, we might find illicit lovers, finally alone together, being interrupted right before the first kiss by the unexpected return of the woman's husband, which leads to the dude having to hide in the closet in his underwear, which leads to the woman having to explain away to her husband the presence of her lover's trousers under the bed, which leads to the husband trying to make love to her, which leads to the lover trying to retrieve his clothes without the husband noticing, and so on.

Two plays worth checking out that brilliantly exemplify this – and every other – principle of farce are *A Flea in Her Ear* and *What the Butler Saw*.

French playwright Georges Feydeau (1862–1921), widely considered to be the father of modern farce, wrote tons of these bedroom farces, full of convenient inconveniences and surprises. *A Flea in Her Ear* (see what he did there?) is a *tour de force* of sex, violence, mistaken identity, lies, and deceit, all played at a breakneck pace with witty dialogue that still elicits laughter from a modern audience.

English playwright Joe Orton (1933–1967), whose life was tragically cut short, was a modern comedic genius. His still oft-performed *What the Butler Saw* is nothing short of a master class in farce.

Pace and Timing

In farce, a rapid dialogue pace is usually required to keep the momentum of the story going and to stay ahead of the audience. So, directors must make sure that the actors pick up their cues! Look at screwball comedies from the 1940s: the dialogue was often delivered at light speed, yet in the hands of great actors like Cary Grant and Rosalind Russell, the stars of *His Girl Friday*, it was acted seemed effortless. That precision, however, was the result of many hours of repetitive rehearsal, so don't be shy about having the actors run the lines over and over until they are razor-sharp.

Also, for the love of all that is good and true in the world, in live performance, make sure that the actors *hold for laughs*. In live comedy, most of the pauses should be created by the audience's laughter. So, the actors must *hold* until the laugh dies down before going on with the dialogue, otherwise they will lose the audience's trust. An audience will always prioritize following the story, so if they think they will miss essential dialogue because the actors are speaking over their laughter, they'll stop laughing. So, the actors need to hold the moment until the house is more or less silent, otherwise all the directorial work you've done to make the comedy play will be for naught and you'll get very cranky. Holding for laughs is an essential piece of comedic stagecraft.

Which brings us to *timing*.

Timing. Ah, timing. It's kind of hard to explain, but comic timing does exist and some folks are born with it, which is not to say that an actor can't improve with experience. In terms of dialogue, timing is mostly centered on how to deliver the punch line, which means knowing when and how long to pause in order to create suspense in the audience. A punch line resolves a thought, but not how the audience thought it was going to be resolved. So, the actor might need to hold a pause long enough for the audience to formulate an idea of what the end of the thought might be, and then hit them with the surprise, that is, the punch line. On the other hand, if the actor pauses too long, the audience might get ahead of them, or the energy of the moment might dissipate. But always remember that that the punch line is the *point* the character is trying to make, not just an excuse to be funny.

Sometimes an actor needs to play with a line to find the correct timing, and often, as the director, you don't know what timing really works until you get in front of a live audience, but believe me, the audience will tell you what is and isn't working right away. And here's the brutal truth: if the writing isn't funny, there's not a whole lot you can do about it. As I learned many years ago, "If it ain't on the page, it ain't on the stage."

Pace and timing aren't always about speed. Sometimes a long pause creates a great comedic moment. Check out Jim Carrey's first transition from docile dorrmat Charlie to Hank, his badass cop alter ego in *Me, Myself & Irene*. Back in the day, Jackie Gleason as Ralph Kramden in *The Honeymooners* perfected what is now referred to as "the slow burn." Something would happen that would make Ralph angry, and Gleason would allow the tension to build and build as he tried to control himself until he finally exploded in a fit of rage, which was often counterbalanced by his wife Alice's utterly nonplussed reaction.

Regarding pace, the director must think in terms of *dynamics*. A director's knowledge of when to slow down, when to pause, and when to pick up the pace is essential to the execution of comedic scenes, whether they are purely dialogue or full of sight gags and physical humor.

All this said, timing is something the performer finds through experience; a director can only explain so much. (Good night, everyone. Thanks for coming to my TED Talk.) But here's a technical trick that quickly solves a lot of problems with landing punch lines: make sure that the actors *speak to end of the line*. The funny part of a line comes at the end, and sometimes it doesn't land in the audience's ear simply because the actor has run out of breath and the end of the line gets lost.

A battle-tested tool for getting actors to keep the pace up is the aforementioned *speed through*. A speed through or two before rehearsing a scene is a great warm-up and further instills the habit of keeping the pace up. I suggest doing them even in run throughs; if there's time, do a speed through of the entire script before running the play.

Examples of Pace and Timing
- *Moonlighting* (Bruce Willis and Cybill Shepherd's constant bantering)
- *His Girl Friday* (Cary Grant and Rosalind Russell)

- *Some Like It Hot* (Jack Lemmon, Tony Curtis, and Marilyn Monroe)
- *It Happened One Night* (Clark Gable and Claudette Colbert)
- *The West Wing* ("walk and talk" scenes)

Sudden Transitions

Sudden transitions are executed by the actor on stage, although in film the timing can be manipulated via editing. The principle works best when going from one moment to an entirely *different* moment quickly, clearly and, sharply. It might be a beat (action) change. It might be a tactic (tool) change. It ultimately doesn't matter which – the actor needs to JUST DO IT! Execute!

Juxtaposing radically different moments together also helps the actor to create the *illusion* of surprise, and the good director knows that's where the laugh is.

Examples

- Kramer's entrances in *Seinfeld*. He's the king of being taken aback, often by nothing at all.
- John Belushi suddenly destroys a whiny, sappy singer's guitar in *Animal House*.
- *Old School*: Frank the Tank (Will Ferrell) accidentally shoots himself in the neck with a tranq gun.
- *Road Trip*: The prostate milking scene.

Hostile Physical Environment (and Its Opposite)

As we've discussed, the physical universe of farce is violent and unpredictable, and often the laws of physics themselves are suspended. The Road Runner can walk on air between two cliffs, but Wile E. Coyote cannot (or even worse, he runs out of steam halfway across – damn you again, Chuck Jones!). The principle at work here is that, in farce, the physical world itself often acts as an antagonist: the protagonist is faced with a series of physical obstacles that they are ill-equipped to cope with. Nemeses include inhospitable weather, common mechanical and household objects, technology, and decrepit dwellings, all of which are made exponentially more difficult when characters find themselves in unfamiliar surroundings.

Examples

- Anywhere Inspector Clouseau shows up in the *Pink Panther* films (a mansion, a study, a street, a castle with a moat, etc.)[5]
- *Home Alone*: the house (for the bad guys)
- *I Love Lucy*: the candy factory, the vineyard, and many others
- The work of Buster Keaton: train tracks, a building site, a staircase, an outdoor clothesline, a water tower, a staircase, etc.; there was nothing that Keaton's wild imagination could not turn into a sight gag

There is also a directly opposite corollary regarding the physical world in farce: sometimes the environment is ridiculously helpful, and whatever a character needs magically appears or is quickly accessible. For instance, in the "bush reveal" scene in *Scary Movie*, an electric hedge trimmer and plastic goggles magically appear in the guy's hands, and he sets about giving the pretty girl in his bed a much-needed Brazilian trim. Also, *The Monkees* TV show from the 1960s is full of brilliant, surrealist gags where objects magically appear at just the right (or wrong) moment. Micky gets an idea, Peter happens to have a lit light bulb that he puts over Micky's head. That sort of thing.

Stuffing: Precise Staging and Story Relevance

Farce means "to stuff" in French. (Imagine my disappointment to learn that *canard farci* doesn't mean "funny duck" in French.) Once the groundwork of the scene has been correctly laid, the director can then begin to stuff the scene with proper bits of business. And here's where comedy directors really earn their keep: everything in the staging of a farce, even the purely comedic set pieces, must be *ultraprecise* and conceived without sacrificing the integrity of the scene. All shtick must have its basis in action and circumstance. Once again: gratuitous bits cheapen the scene and ultimately alienate the audience because they get the message that the players and director do not respect the story or the characters. And that means the audience will laugh less. A *lot* less. That said, in pure farce, every opportunity for humor is exploited, but the director must decide if a bit ultimately detracts from the story or not.

Examples

- *Modern Times*: the factory scene (Charlie Chaplin)
- *Noises Off*: Act II, almost no dialogue (play by Michael Frayn)
- *Mrs. Doubtfire*: the drunk dinner scene
- *Sleeper*: the opening scene
- *Bridesmaids*: the pooping scene
- *There's Something About Mary*: the dog electrocution scene
- *A Night at the Opera*: The stateroom scene (Marx Brothers)
- *The Cable Guy*: the fight at Medieval Times
- *Broadcast News*: the tape delivery scene (Joan Cusack crushes this one!)
- *This is Spinal Tap*: Stonehenge concert
- *Raising Arizona*: the chase scene
- *Galaxy Quest*: the fight between Jason Nesmith (Tim Allen) and the rock monster

A Practical Aesthetics Approach to Analyzing Farce

In farce, what characters see as correct actions are often a result of the skewed perspective: their worldviews, and thus their desires, are *out of adjustment* to what most people would agree upon as being socially acceptable. So when analyzing scenes in comedy, the director must design the actions to solve the problem at hand from the character's point of view rather than self-consciously amp up the humor (i.e., the actions must be *nonmanipulative*).

The inverted thinking of "big things made small, small things made big" is super helpful in comedic text analysis. What might be a matter of insignificance to a character in a drama might be a matter of life and death to a character in a farce (or vice versa).

Even though *Pulp Fiction* is a dark comedy, let's analyze the "I shot Marvin in the face" scene according to the rules of farce, which are completely applicable.

Vincent

1. Vincent is literally making it clear to Jules that he shot Marvin by accident.
2. Action: Get a bro to take a minor mishap in stride.

Jules
1. Jules is literally bitching Vincent out for shooting Marvin.
2. Action: Demand a careless dumbshit fix his screwup.

This simple analysis takes into account many of the tropes of farce: it trivializes an otherwise horrific event (big made small), it renders an act of violence palatable to the audience, it takes the situation seriously from the characters' points of view, and finally, it embraces an utterly skewed perspective. So now we have a good basis with which to rehearse the scene.

The Rehearsal Process

The rehearsal sequence for farce is basically the same as for drama, with a few differences in emphasis.

1. *Director's preparation.* In your preparation, you'll find the principles in this chapter very useful. When you think about the themes, Unifying Principle, etc., look at the deeper values of the story, whatever they might be. Ask yourself who and/or what the writer is targeting – what sacred cows are being roasted? What larger point is the story making about the foibles of human nature? The answers to these questions will form the basis of your approach to the material and help you find your Unifying Principle.
2. *First read through.* The same deal as we've already discussed. Have fun, make sure the actors speak up, and relieve them of the obligation to be funny. You don't want them pushing for laughs from the get-go because that is a hard habit to break. Just hear the play and have a good time.
3. *Discussion.* Approach the material like a drama. At the outset, forget about all the funny stuff. Discuss the thematic implications you've worked on in your preparation. Help the actors find the *truth* of their characters, and the comedy will then flow organically.
4. *First scene rehearsals.* Impart to the actors what the "serious" actions are. Remember what Mel Brooks said – the *situation* is

absurd, but the actors have to play it straight. Without the truth, there is no comedy. Once these values are established, you can begin to tease out the humor. Farce is a highly theatrical construct, so if the actors are missing moments of humor, well, that's a problem. Here's a bit of Zen advice for you: make sure the actors know where the jokes are so they can forget about them. (Meditate on that, grasshopper.)

5. *Blocking.* All the mechanics of good staging apply. You might have some notes about moments or bits, and that's fine. The key here is to work slowly and meticulously. Physical comedy in particular must have a martial precision that still looks completely natural. We had a saying back at my old dojo: "Work slow, learn fast." So, work specifically moment to moment and give the actors as much repetitive practice as your rehearsal schedule will allow. Technique aside, try stuff! If something doesn't work, who cares? Move on and try something else. Remember that as a director, you have a certain amount of latitude in staging a comedy, because the physical life of the scene, with very few exceptions, is not going to be completely specified by the writer. But if the conflict of the scene and the actor's intentions are your North Star, you'll be mindful to only include what's organic to the scene. That said, use your imagination! Play!

6. *Later rehearsals and run throughs.* Comedy is, in many ways, more technically demanding than drama. Stagecraft is key here; the actors must be extremely disciplined in their execution. This is where you will concentrate most of your energy as a director, so get on your feet as soon as possible so you have plenty of time to refine the delivery of every scene. Speed throughs are also super helpful – pace, pace, pace! Do as many speed throughs as you can!

It's worth revisiting the notion that in comedy there is a real tendency for the actors to start to push for laughs in later rehearsals, because after rehearsing a bit or piece of dialogue over and over, those moments don't feel funny anymore. Dress rehearsals and previews will bring those beats back to life and also tell you what is and is not working. You'll find that things tend to fall apart if the actors get lazy or sloppy in their execution, so you must lovingly demand that they stay on point. And if a piece of staging that you were convinced would bring the house down in rehearsal lays there like a dead fish in performance, fix it.

Then, give it over to the actors; tell them to hoist the Jolly Roger and make the thing their own pirate ship. Then pray to the Gods of Comedy to bless the lot of you.

Conclusion: Political Correctness and the Death of Comedy

Great comedy is often about speaking truth to power. By its nature, comedy is provocative and transgressive. The old and still eminently useful trope of comedy as "the angry art" still persists in farce and satire – make 'em laugh in their seats, and they just might think about what's wrong with the world on the drive home. Great stand-up comics know this: whether their bag is observational, political, absurdist, or what have you, they are willing to call society out on its never-ending supply of bullshit. Great comedy writers and directors do not hesitate to offend people who need to be offended, and neither should you. But where do you draw the line?

If comedy writers are tied up in knots with worry over offending people, they will never write anything worthwhile. They will never find their voices or their truth. Political correctness is a form of censorship that demands that the artist adhere to someone else's imposed standards, and that is tantamount to putting a stranglehold on any form of creativity. But as noted in the opening chapters, as society changes, certain things are, for good reason, no longer acceptable and, in the case of comedy, just not funny anymore. In current parlance, "punching down," always the cheapest way to get a laugh, is just not cool. (Simply put, "punching down" is attacking someone, usually a member of a disenfranchised group, who has less power in a given situation and therefore cannot adequately defend themself.)

Not sure if you're punching down or not? Then ask yourself what the joke is. What's the punch line? Is the *payoff* the fact that the butt of the joke is gay? Black? Jewish? Handicapped? A woman? If that's the extent of the humor, then the joke is probably punching in the wrong direction. Remember: great satire attacks people for what they *do*, not what they *are*. So, if you're going to do comedy that's pointed and relevant, you must make peace with the fact that someone is probably going to be offended or, at the very least, not find it funny. That's perfectly okay, but don't let that stop you from trusting your own instincts and taking a big shot. You can't please everyone, so you might as well say what you want to say; if you have a worthy target, lock, load and let 'em have it. Don't be afraid of politically motivated criticism, or more importantly, your own opinions. Go after the big fish. You'll thank me for it one day.

And finally, funny for funny's sake, with no agenda other than to make people laugh, is perfectly okay. We need some of that in the world, too.

Exercise

Watch the following films and TV shows – or any others you like – and write down examples of the farce principles as they occur. Make sure your remote has fresh batteries.

1. *Fawlty Towers*: "The Germans" episode
2. *The Good Place*: "Rhonda, Diana, Jake, and Trent" episode
3. *30 Rock*: "The Bubble" episode
4. *The Lego Batman Movie* (animated film)
5. *Californication*: "The Apartment" episode

Farce Principles Checklist

1. Play it straight
2. Base appetites and shamelessness
3. Indestructibility (violence rendered painless)
4. Big things made small, small things made big
5. Rising complications and the unexpected
6. Pace and timing
7. Sudden transitions
8. The skewed perspective (actions)
9. Hostile physical environment
10. Helpful physical environment
11. Stuffing

Notes

1 Fish out of water examples: *Some Like It Hot, My Cousin Vinnie, Sleeper, Beverly Hills Cop, Pleasantville.*)
2 The rules are somewhat different when it comes to the chief antagonist or certain minor characters. Although perhaps irredeemable, they need not elicit our empathy or change much, if at all; rather, they need to engage our fascination.

3   This was in fact the case: *Fail Safe*, directed by Sidney Lumet and starring Henry Fonda and Walter Matthau, has the exact same plot, and it works brilliantly as a thriller.
4   Check out the "Scott's Tots" episode. You won't ever find a more agonizingly uncomfortable half-hour of television comedy.
5   Peter Sellers and writer-director Blake Edwards are two of the great cinematic masters of sight gags. I suggest you watch all of the *Pink Panther* films. The best one is *The Return of the Pink Panther*.

Appendix

Other Comedy Genres

What follows is a very brief overview of a few other prevalent comedy styles. They differ from farce, but, in practice, their defining characteristics derive from the selective use of certain farce principles while diminishing or disregarding others.

Parody

Parody is an affectionate send-up of the source material and often includes mimicry and meticulously recreated visual elements. Parody largely depends on the audience's ability to identify with the source material, although select elements are often exaggerated for increased comedic effect. Targets of parody include film, TV, music, actors, musicians, public figures, literary works, artworks, etc.

- *Love and Death*: Written and directed by Woody Allen, this film is a send-up of both great Russian novels like *War and Peace* and epic films set in Russia such as *Dr. Zhivago*. A great example of visual gags and other absurdities executed within a serious framework.
- *The Complete Works of William Shakespeare (Abridged)*: This hilarious theatrical send-up of Shakespeare by Adam Long, Daniel Singer, and Jess Winfield finds a trio of actors performing at least a snippet of every one of Shakespeare's plays in less than two hours. The second act is a fast and furious version of *Hamlet*, but the first act pokes good-natured fun at many of Shakespeare's best-known conceits, including the fact that all of his comedies have, more or less, the same plot.
- *Crazy Ex-Girlfriend*: Although the show itself may not be, in the strictest sense, a parody, the musical numbers that pepper every

episode are dead-on examples of the parody genre, ranging from Beyoncé, to boy bands, to Marilyn Monroe, to Fred Astaire, to 1980s pop, to rap battles. The numbers often function on two levels, both effortlessly mimicking the styles they're poking fun at and also using those conventions to comment on the mental and emotional states of the characters in the larger story.
- *Jimmy Fallon's parody of The Doors*. Fallon's Tonight Show sketch finds the intense 60s band performing the theme song from the kid's show "Reading Rainbow" in the style of "Light My Fire", which the Doors actually performed on the Ed Sullivan Show. The visual and musical recreations are dead-on, as is Fallon's uncanny impersonation of singer Jim Morrison.

Satire

Satire differs from parody in both tone and intention. Satire uses ridicule, irony, and exaggeration to make fun of, expose, and criticize what the writer sees as a form of vice, hypocrisy, foolishness, corruption, or immorality. Its targets are often the same as those of parody, but satire is not affectionate toward its subject matter. Satire often veers into dark comedy, but its intent is to provoke both thought and laughter, even outrage, from the audience.

- *The Great Dictator*: Charlie Chaplin's masterpiece functions as both a hilariously vicious send-up of Adolph Hitler and a plea to humanity for a better, more kind and just world.
- *Veep*: This television satire, created by Armando Ianucci, starring the brilliant Julia Louis-Dreyfus and a first-rate supporting cast, satirizes politics and social fabric of Washington, D.C. The main satirical thrust of the show is that our leaders are all too human, which means that they are largely clueless.
- *The Accidental Death of an Anarchist*: Dario Fo's seminal theatrical satire uses elements of farce and slapstick to lampoon authoritarian governments and their pathetic attempts to cover up their misdeeds, which include torture and defenstration.

Black Comedy

Black comedy is both horrific and funny at the same time. The genre is characterized by extreme violence, disregard of social norms, and amoral, often sociopathic characters. Black comedy also violates, by design, some of the basic rules of comedy in that characters often suffer more realistically, but it's still, somehow, absurdly funny. It is arguably the most difficult of all comedy genres because the balancing act between comedy and dark drama is extremely delicate.

It's worth mentioning that much of Key and Peele's sketch material deftly manages a very difficult trick: to move from light to dark, yet maintain cohesiveness in the writing and performing. A particularly vivid example is the "Aerobics Contest." What begins as a silly, dead-accurate parody of 1980s aerobics competitions takes a sharp turn when one of the contestants is told via cue cards that his family has been killed in a car crash. Because he's on a live show, he is forced to keep up the aerobics routine and maintain a smile on his face as he digests the increasingly tragic news, much to the delight of his likely complicit competitor. It's both very funny and deeply disquieting. Kind of brilliant, if you ask me.

- *Barry*: An award-winning HBO comedy about a hitman for hire (the talented Bill Hader in the titular role) who discovers a love for acting and tries to get out of his old life. However, his manipulative business partner (Stephen Root) and the Chechen mob have different ideas, which forces Barry to resort to what he's really good at: killing people. An effective mix of dark and light, supported by the characters and the circumstances.
- *Mr. Burns: A Post-Electric Play*: Anna Washburn's postapocalyptic dark comedy uses an episode of *The Simpsons* as a means of exploring how stories both survive and change from generation to generation.

Comedy-Drama (Dramedy)

My least favorite word in the English language is dramedy, but it's useful as a working definition. Dramedy implies a realistic, naturalistic situation that deals with serious issues, but the material is imbued with humor. The form finds humor in everyday situations, and the characters often consciously use humor as a coping mechanism. Dramedy often employs a tragic plot but with a happy or bittersweet ending. This subgenre is generally a comedy with dramatic moments, although the argument for the reverse is often made.

- *Juno*: Diablo Cody's funny and moving tale of a rebellious teenager who, after getting pregnant, decides to take the baby to term and then put it up for adoption.
- *Fleabag*: Phoebe Waller-Bridge created, wrote, and starred in this provocative television comedy about a free-spirited, sexually active, but lonely woman who is trying to put her life back together after a terrible loss. A great example of using the principles of comedy-drama to provide the audience with a wide range of emotional experiences.
- *In the Next Room (or The Vibrator Play)*: Sarah Ruhl's period drama about women seeking medical care for hysteria who are treated with a vibrator to, ostensibly, release toxic fluids from their uterus. This causes the patients to, for the first time, experience intense orgasms, which opens the door for the play to explore themes of female sexuality and society's repression of female sexual desire.
- *High Maintenance*: Created by the ex-husband and wife team of Ben Sinclair and Katja Blichfeld, this anthology series follows an unnamed character simply known as The Guy (Sinclair) as he delivers weed on his bicycle to his various clients, mostly in ethnically diverse Brooklyn, New York. While occasionally funny, the show is less concerned with getting laughs and more centered on generating narrative snapshots of the characters' loneliness, sense of disconnection, and longing for fuller lives.

Final Note

In comedy, there is much crossover; for instance, a black comedy can also function as a satire, and so on. These genre distinctions are simply meant to clarify the stylistic differences in various forms of popular comedy.

Works Cited

The 40 Year Old Virgin. Directed by Judd Apatow. Universal Pictures, 2005.
Animal Crackers. Directed by Victor Heerman. Paramount Pictures, 1930.
Bad Santa. Directed by Terry Zwigoff. Miramax, 2003.
Barry. Created by Alec Berg and Bill Hader. HBO, 2018. Television.
Bentley, Eric. *The Life of the Drama*. New York, Applause Theatre Books, 1991.

Borgeson, Jess, et al. *The Complete Works of William Shakespeare (Abridged)*. London, New York, Applause, 2012.
Bridesmaids. Directed by Paul Feig. Universal Pictures, 2011.
Broadcast News. Directed by James L. Brooks. Twentieth Century Fox, 1987.
The Cable Guy. Directed by Ben Stiller. Columbia Pictures, 1996.
The Cocoanuts. Directed by Robert Florey and Joseph Santley. Paramount Pictures, 1929.
Crazy Ex-Girlfriend. Created by Rachel Bloom and Aline Brosh McKenna. The CW Network, 2015. Television.
Darrach, Brad. "Mel Brooks Playboy Interview." *Playboy*, February 1975.
Dodgeball: A True Underdog Story. Directed by Rawson Marshall Thurber. Twentieth Century Fox, 2004.
Dr. Strangelove or: How I Learned to Stop Worrying and Love the Bomb. Directed by Stanley Kubrick. Columbia Pictures, 1964.
Duck Soup. Directed by Leo McCarey. Paramount Pictures, 1933.
Feydeau, Georges, et al. *A Flea in Her Ear*. London, Oberon Books, 2010.
Fleabag. Created by Phoebe Waller-Bridge. Amazon Prime Video, 2016. Television.
Fo, Dario, et al. *The Accidental Death of an Anarchist*. London, Methuen Drama, 2009.
Frayn, Michael. *Noises Off: A Play in Three Acts*. London, Methuen Drama, 2012.
Freud, Sigmund, and James Strachey. *Jokes and Their Relation to the Unconscious, Vol. 8*. New York, Norton, 1960.
Galaxy Quest. Directed by Dean Parisot. Dreamworks Pictures, 1999.
Ghostbusters. Directed by Ivan Reitman. Columbia Pictures, 1984.
The Great Dictator. Directed by Charles Chaplin. United Artists, 1940.
High Maintenance. Created by Ben Sinclair and Katja Blichfeld. HBO, 2016. Television.
His Girl Friday. Directed by Howard Hawks. Columbia Pictures, 1940.
Home Alone. Directed by Chris Columbus. Twentieth Century Fox, 1990.
The Honeymooners. Created by Jackie Gleason. CBS, 1955. Television.
Horse Feathers. Directed by Norman Z. McLeod. Paramount Pictures, 1932.
I Love Lucy. Created by Jess Oppenheimer. CBS, 1951. Television.
In Living Color. Created by Keenen Ivory Wayans. 20th Century Fox Television, 1990. Television.
In the Loop. Directed by Armando Iannucci. IFC Films, 2009.
Juno. Directed by Jason Reitman. Fox Searchlight Pictures, 2007.
Key and Peele. Created by Keegan-Michael Key and Jordan Peele. Comedy Central, 2012. Television.
The Killer Inside Me. Directed by Michael Winterbottom. IFC Films, 2010.
The Lady Eve. Directed by Preston Sturges. Paramount Pictures, 1941.
Love and Death. Directed by Woody Allen. United Artists, 1975.
Me, Myself & Irene. Directed by Bobby Farrelly and Peter Farrelly. Twentieth Century Fox, 2000.
Modern Times. Directed by Charlie Chapin. United Artists, 1936.
The Monkees. Created by Paul Mazursky and Larry Tucker. NBC, 1966. Television.
Monty Python and the Holy Grail. Directed by Terry Gilliam and Terry Jones. Cinema 5 Distributing, 1975.
Monty Python's Flying Circus. BBC TV, 1969. Television.
Mrs. Doubtfire. Directed by Chris Columbus. Twentieth Century Fox, 1993.
National Lampoon's Animal House. Directed by John Landis. Universal Pictures, 1978.
National Lampoon's Vacation. Directed by Harold Ramis. Warner Bros., 1983.
The Nice Guys. Directed by Shane Black. Warner Bros., 2016.
The Office. Created by Greg Daniels, Ricky Gervais, and Stephen Merchant. NBC, 2005. Television.

A Night at the Opera. Directed by Sam Wood. MGM, 1935
Old School. Directed by Todd Phillips. Dreamworks, 2003
Orton, Joe. *What the Butler Saw*. London, Methuen Drama, 2000.
Pulp Fiction. Directed by Quentin Tarantino. Miramax, 1994.
Raising Arizona. Directed by Joel Coen. Twentieth Century Fox, 1987.
The Return of the Pink Panther. Directed by Blake Edwards. United Artists, 1975.
Ruhl, Sarah. *In the Next Room (or The Vibrator Play)*. New York, Theatre Communications Group, 2016.
Saturday Night Live. Created by Lorne Michaels. NBC, 1975. Television.
Scary Movie. Directed by Keenen Ivory Wayans. Dimension Films, 2000.
Seinfeld. Created by Larry David and Jerry Seinfeld. NBC, 1989. Television.
Serial Mom. Directed by John Waters. Savoy Pictures, 1994.
Sleeper. Directed by Woody Allen. United Artists, 1973.
The Sopranos. Created by David Chase. HBO, 1999. Television.
There's Something About Mary. Directed by Bobby Farrelly and Peter Farrelly. Twentieth Century Fox, 1998.
This is Spinal Tap. Directed by Rob Reiner. Embassy Pictures, 1984.
The Tonight Show Starring Jimmy Fallon. Created by Steve Allen, Dwight Hemion, William O. Harbach, Sylvester "Pat" Weaver. NBC, 2014.
Tropic Thunder. Directed by Ben Stiller. DreamWorks, 2008.
Unbreakable Kimmy Schmidt. Created by Robert Carlock and Tina Fey. Netflix, 2015. Television.
Veep. Created by Armando Ianucci. HBO, 2012. Television.
Warner Bros. Cartoons (Bugs Bunny, Daffy Duck et al). Warner Bros., 1926.
Washburn, Anne, and Almeida Theatre (London, England). *Mr. Burns: A Post-Electric Play*. London, Oberon Books, 2016.
Young Frankenstein. Directed by Mel Brooks. Twentieth Century Fox, 1974.

11
Conclusion

Good writers and directors know when to wrap it up. So here we are.

Working with actors is great fun, and when you see your babies up onstage kicking butt, you can't help but feel like a proud mama or papa. But like any good parent, you have to know when to let go. The thing will never be exactly as you imagined it, and once you not only accept but *embrace* that fact, there are many good times ahead.

Leadership is a strange beast. I have always been deeply mistrustful of authority, which is ironic because I've spent most of my adult life in a position of leadership – teacher, director, producer, etc. What I've learned is that as a director, you have to let go of your ego, but also steer the ship. *You* have the final say in terms of what is required from the actors, and the best ones will tell you – Jack Nicholson comes immediately to mind – that the actor's job is to serve the vision of the director. This is why we spent so much time on understanding a text and allowing our point of view to guide all of the production's aesthetic choices, and that includes the actors' performances.

You don't have to be a dictator, and as we discussed, you want to create a safe environment where everyone's ideas are valued. But you must decide when the conversation is over and how things are going to go. If an actor is unwilling or unable to accommodate your instructions, then they are either not skilled enough to play the role or simply suffering from a bit of anxiety, which you now have some tools to help them cope with. Remember: the anxiety actors feel about the scene *is* the scene. So, use the rehearsals to help them channel that energy into the work – there's gold in them thar hills.

In rehearsal, as much as you've prepared, you, director-person, need to be in the moment as much as the actors; that's the only way to recognize and nurture a great moment. Once you've prepared, don't overthink it. Trust your *instincts* in rehearsal, knowing that you will be guided by your preparation. You'll also save yourself, and everyone else, a lot of grief if you abide by this simple axiom:

If it ain't broke, don't fix it.

Thank you for taking the time to read this book. I hope it helps you find your own groove as a director, and makes the process of working with actors a joyful one. I leave you with the words of Willie the Shakes, whose thoughts on acting still ring true.

Hamlet's Advice to the Players
Hamlet:
> *Speak the speech, I pray you, as I pronounced it to you, trippingly on the tongue: but if you mouth it, as many of your players do, I had as lief the town-crier spoke my lines. Nor do not saw the air too much with your hand, thus, but use all gently; for in the very torrent, tempest, and, as I may say, the whirlwind of passion, you must acquire and beget a temperance that may give it smoothness. O, it offends me to the soul to hear a robustious periwig-pated fellow tear a passion to tatters, to very rags, to split the ears of the groundlings, who for the most part are capable of nothing but inexplicable dumbshows and noise: I would have such a fellow whipped for o'erdoing Termagant; it*

out-herods Herod: pray you, avoid it.
Be not too tame neither, but let your own discretion
be your tutor: suit the action to the word, the
word to the action; with this special o'erstep not
the modesty of nature: for any thing so overdone is
from the purpose of playing, whose end, both at the
first and now, was and is, to hold, as 'twere, the
mirror up to nature; to show virtue her own feature,
scorn her own image, and the very age and body of
the time his form and pressure. Now this overdone,
or come tardy off, though it make the unskilful
laugh, cannot but make the judicious grieve; the
censure of the which one must in your allowance
o'erweigh a whole theatre of others. O, there be
players that I have seen play, and heard others
praise, and that highly, not to speak it profanely,
that, neither having the accent of Christians nor
the gait of Christian, pagan, nor man, have so
strutted and bellowed that I have thought some of
nature's journeymen had made men and not made them
well, they imitated humanity so abominably.

First Player:

I hope we have reformed that indifferently with us, sir.

Hamlet:

O, reform it altogether. And let those that play
your clowns speak no more than is set down for them;
for there be of them that will themselves laugh, to
set on some quantity of barren spectators to laugh
too; though, in the mean time, some necessary
question of the play be then to be considered:
that's villainous, and shows a most pitiful ambition
in the fool that uses it. Go, make you ready.

True dat.

Peace. Out.

Works Cited

Shakespeare, William. "Hamlet: Prince of Denmark." In *Riverside Shakespeare*. Boston, Houghton Mifflin Company, 1973.

Suggested Reading and Viewing

Plays (alphabetized by author)
- *Who's Afraid of Virginia Woolf?* by Edward Albee
- *Waiting for Godot* by Samuel Beckett
- *Speed-the-Plow* by David Mamet
- *Death of a Salesman* by Arthur Miller
- *In the Next Room (or The Vibrator Play)* by Sarah Ruhl
- *For Colored Girls Who Have Considered Suicide/When the Rainbow is Enuf* by Ntozake Shange
- *The Curious Incident of the Dog in the Night-Time* by Simon Stephens
- *How I Learned to Drive* by Paula Vogel
- *The Importance of Being Earnest* by Oscar Wilde
- *A Streetcar Named Desire* by Tennessee Williams
- *Fences* by August Wilson

Shakespeare
- *Henry V*
- *Macbeth*
- *The Merchant of Venice*
- *Romeo and Juliet*

SUGGESTED READING AND VIEWING

Screenplays (alphabetized by author)
Good Will Hunting by Ben Affleck and Matt Damon
Carnal Knowledge by Jules Pfeiffer
A Few Good Men by Aaron Sorkin
Chinatown by Robert Towne

Books (alphabetized by author)
The Life of the Drama by Eric Bentley
Farce: A History From Aristophanes to Woody Allen by Albert Bermel
The Empty Space by Peter Brook
A Practical Handbook for the Actor by Melissa Bruder, Lee Michael Cohn, et al.
Acting in Film by Michael Caine
Actions: The Actors' Thesaurus by Marina Calderone and Maggie Lloyd-Williams
The Art of Dramatic Writing by Lagos Egri
Jokes and Their Relation to the Unconscious by Sigmund Freud
The Three Uses of the Knife by David Mamet
True and False by David Mamet
Dialogue by Robert McKee
Story by Robert McKee
Writing the Pilot by William Rabkin
Rewrites: A Memoir by Neil Simon

Films (alphabetized by title)
Abbott and Costello Meet Frankenstein
American Graffiti
The Band's Visit
Carnal Knowledge
Carrie
Chinatown
Dangerous Liaisons
Dirty Harry
Duck Soup
Fences
A Few Good Men

The Four Musketeers (1974, Richard Lester, director)
The General
Get Out
Ghostbusters
Good Will Hunting
Henry V (Branagh)
Henry V (Olivier)
L.A. Confidential
The Lady Eve
Lawrence of Arabia
Looking for Richard
Modern Times
Moonlight
Munich
Parasite
The Reader
Return of the Pink Panther
Rocky
The Searchers
Spider-Man (2002, Sam Raimi, director)
Tender Mercies
The Three Musketeers (1973, Richard Lester, director)
Who's Afraid of Virginia Woolf?
The Wizard of Oz

TV (alphabetized by title)

Acting in Film with Michael Caine. BBC
Dexter. Showtime Networks
The Mahabarata (Peter Brook). BBC
A Midsummer Night's Dream with Peter Brook. BBC
Playing Shakespeare. BBC

Examples of Farce

Plays (alphabetized by author)

Lysistrata by Aristophanes
Taking Steps, Absurd Person Singular, Round and Round the Garden, Bedroom Farce, How the Other Half Loves, and others by Alan Ayckbourn

Boeing-Boeing by Marc Camoletti
The Suicide and The Mandate by Nikolai Erdmann
A Flea in Her Ear, Hotel Paradiso, and *A Little Hotel on the Side* by Georges Feydeau
The Accidental Death of an Anarchist by Dario Fo
Noises Off by Michael Frayn
The Play That Goes Wrong by Henry Lewis, Henry Shields, and Jonathan Sayer
Lend Me a Tenor by Ken Ludwig
The Ritz by Terrence McNally
Tartuffe, Learned Ladies, The Misanthrope, School for Husbands, and *School for Wives* by Molière
What the Butler Saw and *Loot* by Joe Orton
Black Comedy by Peter Schaffer

Films (alphabetized by title)

Airplane!
Anchorman
Animal House
Billy Madison
The Birdcage
Blazing Saddles
Caddyshack
Dumb and Dumber
A Fish Called Wanda
Harold and Kumar Go to White Castle
History of the World, Part I
Kentucky Fried Movie
The Keystone Kops
The Lego Batman Movie
Marx Brothers films
Monty Python and the Holy Grail
Monty Python's Life of Brian
Naked Gun films
Sleeper
Soapdish

Stripes
There's Something About Mary
Three Stooges films
Up in Smoke (Cheech and Chong)
What's Up, Doc?
Zoolander

TV (alphabetized by title)
30 Rock
Absolutely Fabulous
Brooklyn Nine-Nine
Family Guy
Fawlty Towers
Get Smart
The Good Place
I Love Lucy
Key and Peele
Little Britain
Malcolm in the Middle
Married. . . With Children
Monty Python's Flying Circus
Mork and Mindy
Mr. Show
The Muppet Show
My Name is Earl
Saturday Night Live
Scrubs
SCTV
The Simpsons
Third Rock From the Sun
Unbreakable Kimmy Schmidt
Warner Bros. cartoons
The Young Ones

Index

Note: Page numbers in *italics* indicate a figure on the corresponding page.

12 Angry Men 75
30 Rock 174

absurdity 156, 158
Accidental Death of an Anarchist, The 176
accountability 35
Ackroyd, Dan 160
actable terms 144
Acting in Film (Caine) 133
action-idea 22
actions: acting partner and 34; blocking 124; in camera scripts 116n2; chart of *81*; clarifying 110–111; construction of 33; defining labels 38–40; definition of 32; director's notebook and 80–82; exercises 44–45; fun and 37–38; guidelines for 33–38; importance of 5; list of 40–42; mechanics of 32–38; nonmanipulative 36–37; playable 5, 33, 40–42, 47; "psychophysical" 46–47; purposes of 33; specificity and 38; of the story 25; writer's intentions and 38

actors: connection and 111–112; vulnerability and 109; working with 104
adjustments: checklist 151; emotional 145; pauses 146–147; performance notes 144–145; physical 144–145; preparation 85–86; temperamental 145
adverbs 144–145
"Aerobics Contest" (Key and Peele) 177
Akalaitis, Joanne 17, 18
Albee, Edward 17
Allen, Tim 169
Allen, Woody 175
American Graffiti 10
American Repertory Theatre 17
Anchorman 132
angles 128
Animal Crackers 162
Animal House 168
Ann-Margret 73
Antonioni, Michelangelo 45n2
aphorisms 22–23
Apocalypse Now 73

INDEX

arena stage 122, *122*
Aristotle 22, 47, 152
Art of Dramatic Writing, The (Egri) 22
"As If" memory device 52–62, 64, 82, 110–111, 116n3
As You Like It 18
Atlantic Theater Company 46
audience 13–14

Bad Santa 155
Ball, Lucille 158
Bana, Eric 136
Band's Visit, The 26–27, 28
Barry 177
base appetites 162
Basinger, Kim 126
Batman 72
Battlestar Galactica 75
Baumbach, Noah 45n2
beats: changes 61–62, 77; individual 64, 65, 67, 68
Becket, Samuel 17
Belushi, John 168
Bentley, Eric 157
Benton, Robert 46
Bergen, Candice 73
Bergman, Ingmar 45n2
Bernal, Gael Garcia 135
Berry, Halle 136
Bettelheim, Bruno 47
big things made small 163
black comedy 177
Black Panther 75
Blazing Saddles 154
Blichfeld, Katja 178
blocking the scene: actions and obstacles 124; for comedy 171–172; crosses, positioning, and stillness 127–128; distance and tension 124–127; exercise 137–142; explained 118; physical contact, sex, and violence 130–136; props and business 129–130; purpose of 120; for stage versus camera 118–119; staging principles 123–136
Body Heat 135
Bogart, Anne 18–19
Bolt, Robert 13
Born on the Fourth of July 75
Boston, Rick 67
Branagh, Kenneth 27–28
Brando, Marlon 13
Braveheart 75
Bridesmaids 136, 169
Bridget Jones's Diary 131, 132
Brokeback Mountain 135
Bronx Tale, A 131
Brook, Peter 19, 30n4, 47
Brooks, Mel 158, 171
Buckaroo Banzai 23
Burns, George 32
business 129–130

Caine, Michael 133
Californication 174
Call Me By Your Name 136
Campbell, Joseph 22
cap 34, 54
Capaldi, Peter 161
Carell, Steve 159
Carmen 30n4
Carnal Knowledge 73
Carrey, Jim 158, 166
Carrie 72
cartoons 160, 168
Casino 73
cause and effect 29
Chalamet, Timothée 136
Chan, Jackie 131
Chaplin, Charlie 131, 169, 176
Chase, Chevy 164
cheating out 122, 128
Chinatown 10, 13, 21, 72, 74, 110
"Chocolate and Strawberries" (Diamond and Boston) 67–68
Christie, Julie 135

Churchill, Winston 27
Cleese, John 156
clichés 114–116
Close Encounters of the Third Kind 108
Cocoanuts, The 162
Cody, Diablo 178
Cohn, Lee 108
Colbert, Claudette 167
comedy: Aristotle on 152; benefits of 152–153; black 177; blocking the scene 171–172; comedic premises 155–157; comedy-drama 177–178; exercise 173–174; farce 153–155, 157–170; Freud on 152; parody 175–176; political correctness and 172–173; rehearsal process 171–172; satire 176
comedy-drama 177–178
Complete Works of William Shakespeare (Abridged), The 175–176
conflict: versus confrontation 82; forces in opposition 24–25; necessity of 5
confrontation 82
Connery, Sean 124
contractual issues 30n5
Controlling Idea 23–24, 30n6
Costner, Kevin 130
costumes 85–86
counterpoint 130
Crazy Ex-Girlfriend 176
crosses 127–128
Crowe, Russell 126
Curb Your Enthusiasm 146
Curious Tale of the Dog in the Nighttime, The 73
Curtis, Tony 167

Dangerous Liaisons 115
Daredevil 131
David, Larry 146
Death of a Salesman 11
defining labels 38–40, 42–44
degree of socially unacceptable behavior 154

Dexter 36–37
diagonals 128
dialogue: rehearsals and 112; writer's voice and 20
Diamond, Debbie 67
Die Hard 75
dignity 130
director's notebook: actions 80–82; adjustments and notes 85–86; dramatic event 84–85; key story points 82–84; research 86–98
Dirty Dancing 75
Dirty Harry 23, 26
distance 124–127
Django Unchained 75
Don't Look Now 135
downstage 120
Dragon: The Bruce Lee Story 131
dramatic event 84–85
dramedy 177–178
Dr. Strangelove 157
Drunken Master II 132
Dr. Zhivago 175
Duck Soup 162
Dunst, Kirsten 30n8
duration of socially unacceptable behavior 154
Durning, Charles 147
dynamics 149, 167

early rehearsals: scene rehearsals 107–116; table read 106–107; working with the writer 105–106
Eastern Promises 132
Eat Pray Love 75
Egri, Lagos 22, 23
elixir 22
emotional adjustments 145
emotional memory 54–55
emotional needs 135
emotional state: action and 34–35; inability to perform 6
emotional violence 161

INDEX

Empire Strikes Back, The 83
Empty Space, The 19
Endgame 17
ensemble 128
Equus 74
errand 35–36
Eternal Sunshine of the Spotless Mind 75
Exodus 75
external adjustments 86, 114–116
externalized consequences 56

faking it 32
Falk, Peter 86
farce: base appetites and shamelessness 162; big things made small 163; checklist 174; definition of 153–154; degree of socially unacceptable behavior 154–155; duration of socially unacceptable behavior 154–155; fast transitions 167–168; hostile physical environment 168–169; human suffering in 161–162; indestructible hero 159–162; pace and timing 165–167; playing it straight 157–159; Practical Aesthetics approach 170; principles of 157–170; rehearsal process 171–172; rising complications 164–165; skewed perspective 162–164; small things made big 163–164; stuffing 169–170
Fast Times at Ridgemont High 135
Faulkner, William 158
Fawlty Towers 174
Feldman, Marty 161
Fences 11, 15
Few Good Men, A 16, 82
Feydeau, Georges 165
Ficarra, Glenn 155
Field, Sid 22
fights 131–133
Finding Nemo 75
First Wives Club, The 75
Firth, Peter 131

Fleabag 178
Flea in Her Ear, A 165
Fo, Dario 176
forces in opposition 24–25
For Colored Girls Who Have Considered Suicide/When the Rainbow Is Enuf 29
Ford, John 10
Four Musketeers, The 79n3
Franco, James 30n8
Frayn, Michael 169
Freud, Sigmund 152
Friday the 13th 75
From Russia With Love 131
fun 37–38

Gable, Clark 167
Galaxy Quest 169
Gandhi 75
Garfunkel, Art 73
Gershman-Pitts, Leonora 108
Get Out 10–11
Ghostbusters 163
Glass Menagerie, The 74, 75
Glass, Philip 18
Gleason, Jackie 167
Godfather, The 14
Godfather Part II, The 14
Goldwyn, Samuel 12
Good Place, The 174
Good Will Hunting 56–62, 64, 84–85
Grant, Cary 165, 167
Grant, Hugh 131
Grateful Dead 48
Great Dictator, The 176
Gyllenhaal, Jake 135

habits 103–104
Hader, Bill 177
Hall, Michael C. 36
Hamlet 15, 182–184
Hamm, Jon 136
Hammer, Armie 136
Hanson, Curtis 127

Hatsumi, Masaaki 125
Hauge, Michael 22
Henry IV, Part One 131
Henry V 27–28
High Maintenance 178
His Girl Friday 166, 167
Hoffman, Dustin 147
hold for laughs 166
Home Alone 75, 168
Honeymooners, The 167
Horse Feathers 162
hostile physical environment 168–169
"House of the Rising Sun" 65
How to Succeed in Business Without Really Trying 75
Hunchback of Notre Dame, The 161
Hunter, Kim 13
Hurt, William 135

Ianucci, Armando 176
I Love Lucy 168
imaginative process 53
Immortal Technique 23
Importance of Being Earnest, The 129–130
indestructible hero 159–162
indicating 32, 113
information 12
inherently absurd premise 156
In Living Color 156
Inside Private Lives 108
intention 5
interior life 22
interpretation 13–15
In the Loop 161
In the Next Room 178
intimacy coordinator 133–134
Into the Wild 75
invisible direction 7
It Happened One Night 167
I Wanna Be A Spy 88–98
"I Wonder Who's Kissing Her Now" 66–67

jargon 6
John Wick 75, 131
Jokes and Their Relation to the Unconscious (Freud) 152
Judas and the Black Messiah 75
Jung, Carl 71
Juno 178
Justice For All, And 75
juxtaposition 156

Keaton, Buster 131, 168
Kemper, Ellie 163
Key and Peele 164, 177
key story points 82–84, 111, 123
Kill Bill 131, 132
Killer Inside Me, The 155
Klute 74
Kubrick, Stanley 157

L.A. Confidential 75, 126, 131
Lady Eve, The 75, 157
LaMarr, Phil 163
La Notte 45n2
Lawrence of Arabia 10, 13
leadership 181–182
Ledger, Heath 135
Lee, Bruce 131, 132
Lego Batman Movie, The 174
Leigh, Jennifer Jason 135
Lemmon, Jack 167
Lennon, John 23
lesson learned 22
Lester, Richard 79n3
Lewis, Jerry 158
Life of the Drama, The (Bentley) 157
line readings 113–114
Lloyd, Harold 131
logline 22
Long, Adam 175
Long Day's Journey Into Night 74
Looking for Richard 109
Louis-Dreyfus, Julia 176
Love and Death 175

Lumet, Sidney 46
Lumley, Joanna 158
Luna, Diego 135

Mabou Mines theatre company 18, 30n2
Mad Men 137–142
Maguire, Tobey 30n8
Mahabarata 30n4
Malkovich, John 115
Malmgren, Yat 124
Mamet, David 12, 17, 46, 72, 130
manipulative action 36
Marat/Sade 30n4
Marriage Story 45n2
Marx Brothers 162
McCartney, Paul 23
McKee, Robert 23, 24, 30n6
meaning 13
mechanics of physical action 32–38
Me, Myself & Irene 74, 167
Mendes, Sam 45n2
Merchant of Venice, The 14–15
Method acting 54–55
Method of Physical Acting (Stanislavski) 32, 47
methodologies 16, 104
Midnight Express 75
Midsummer Night's Dream, A 30n4
Miller, Arthur 11
Mississippi Burning 75
model analysis 88–98
Modern Times 169
moment 47
Monkees, The 169
Monroe, Marilyn 167
Monster 73
Monster's Ball 136
Monty Python 159, 161
Monty Python and the Holy Grail 159–160
Monty Python's Flying Circus 156
Moonlight 72
Moonlighting 167
Movement Psychology 124

Mr. Burns: A Post-Electric Play 177
Mrs. Doubtfire 169
Munich 11, 75, 136
Murray, Bill 163

narrative 20
National Lampoon's Vacation 164
nemeses 168
Nichols, Mike 73
Nicholson, Jack 73, 181
Nightmare on Elm Street 75
Nin, Anaïs 15
Noises Off 169
Nolan, Christopher 72
nonlinear forms 28–29
nonnarrative forms 28–29
nonverbal communication 120
Norris, Chuck 132
Now I Ask You 112–113

obstacles: blocking and 124; in story 25, 48, 62, 83–84
"off-book" deadline 119
Office, The 159
Oklahoma! 19, 75
Olivier, Laurence 27
omote 9, 10, 61
One Flew Over the Cuckoo's Nest 75
O'Neill, Eugene 112–113
One Night in Miami 75
opposition 24–25
Orton, Joe 165
overall action 76
"Overly Offended Co-workers" (Key and Peele) 164

pace 149, 165–166
Pacino, Al 109
"paralysis by analysis" 143
Parasite 11
parody 175–176
Patriot, The 75, 132
pauses 146–147, 149–150

Peele, Jordan 10
performance notes 144–145
Phillips, Julia 108
physical adjustments 144–145
physical contact 130–136
Pink Panther 168
Pinter, Harold 146
playable actions 5, 33, 40–42, 47
Playboy (magazine) 158
playing it straight 157–159
plot 10
point of view: of character 49, 76; of director 15–16, 24
political correctness 172–173
positions 127–128
Postcards From the Edge 74
Practical Aesthetics: checklist 62–64; components of 47; farce analysis and 170; overview 46–50; playwright's intentions and 16; scenes 48–50
Practical Handbook for the Actor, A (Bruder, Cohn et al.) 16, 46
premise 22–23
preparation: adjustments 85–86; for comedy 171; delineation of dramatic conflict 48; director's notebook *see* director's notebook; importance of 7; in Practical Aesthetics 48
Primal Need 74–76, 77–78, 98
props 129–130
proscenium arch 120, *121*
psychological state of being 6
"psychophysical" actions 46–47
Pulp Fiction 163, 170
"punching down" 173
pursuit and retreat 124

Rabbit Hole 73
Rabkin, William 10
Raid, The 132
Raimi, Sam 30n8
Rambo 73
Reader, The 23–24

rehearsal process: adjustments 143–147; blocking the scene 118–142; comedy 152–174, 171–172, 175–178; early rehearsals 103–116; run throughs 147–151; sequencing 105
Requa, John 155
research 86–98
resolution of action 25
respect 21
Return of the Pink Panther 160
Revolutionary Road 45n2
Rewrites: A Memoir (Simon) 35
rhythm 146
rising complications 164–165
Rocky 10, 13–14
Rogers and Hammerstein 18–19
Romanus, Robert 135
Romeo and Juliet 25, 28
Royal Shakespeare Company 30n4
Ruhl, Sarah 178
run throughs 147–151, 172
Russell, Rosalind 165, 167

safety 130, 133
satire 176
Saturday Night Live 160
Scarface 75
Scary Movie 169
scene analysis: "As If" memory device 52–62; checklist 62–64; essence of character action 51–52, 63; exercises 64; model of 56–62; Practical Aesthetics approach 48–50; songs to analyze 69; three-step process 50–64; what character is doing 50–51, 62
scene rehearsals 107–116
scenes: nature of 49; structure of 20
Scenes From a Marriage 45n2
Schindler's List 75
Scorsese, Martin 8
Scott Pilgrim vs. the World 132
Searchers, The 10
Secretary 75

Seinfeld 168
Seinfeld, Jerry 146
semantics 37–38
sequencing 105
Serial Mom 164
sex 133–136, 142n2
shadow aspect 71
Shakespeare, William 14–15, 18, 131, 182
shamelessness 162
Shange, Ntozake 29
Shaw, G.B. 15
Shepherd, Cybill 167
sight lines 120, 122
Simon, Neil 35, 157
Simpsons, The 177
sincerity 32
Sinclair, Ben 178
Singer, Daniel 175
Six Degrees of Separation 74
skewed perspective 162–164
Skyfall 72
Sleeper 169
small things made big 163–164
Snoop Dogg 23
Some Like It Hot 167
Sopranos, The 154
Sorkin, Aaron 16
South Pacific 18–19
South Park 11
specificity, of action 38
Speed the Plow 17
speed through 149, 167
Spider-Man 26
Spielberg, Steven 11
Splash 75
stage business 129–130
stagecraft 148, 172
stage directions 112–113
staging: key story points 123; run throughs and 149
Stanislavski, Konstantin 32, 37, 38, 46
"stare-down" 146
Star Is Born, A 75

state of being 6
Steel Magnolias 61
Stiller, Ben 161
stillness 128
story: action of 25; definition of 9; as entertainment/drama 12–13; identifying 21–24; importance of 5; versus plot 10–11; key points 82–84, 111, 123; rehearsals and 111; in table read 107
Story (McKee) 30n6
Straw Dogs 75
Streetcar Named Desire, A 13, 74
stuffing 169–170
Sturges, Preston 157
substitution 52–53
sudden transitions 167–168
suspension of disbelief 86
Sutherland, Donald 135

table reads 106–107, 171
Taken 75
Tandy, Jessica 13
Taps 75
Team America: World Police 136
temperamental adjustments 145
tension 124–127
terminology 120, 122
text: audience interpretation and 12, 13–14; plot 10–11; story 5, 9, 10–11, 12–13, 21–24; theme 11–12, 30n1; Unifying Principle 24–29; writer's intentions and 5, 16–19
theatre-in-the-round 122
theme 11–12, 22, 30n1
There's Something About Mary 161
Thick of It, The 161
This Is Spinal Tap 75
Thornton, Billy Bob 136, 155
Three Musketeers, The 73, 78–79, 79n3
Through-Line Analysis: "As If" memory device 78; essence of character action 78; examples of 78–79, 98–99; exercises

79, 99; explained 76–77; Primal Need 74–76, 77–78; self-awareness and 72–73; three-step process 77–78; what character is doing 77–78; wound 72
thrust stage 120, *121*
Tierno, Michael 22
time management 149
timing 126–127, 166–167
Tommy 72
Tootsie 147
Towne, Robert 13
Travolta, John 163
Turner, Kathleen 135

Unbreakable Kimmy Schmidt 163
underplaying 163
Unforgiven 73
Unifying Principle: examples of 25–28; exercises 29; nonnarrative and nonlinear forms 28–29; real-life examples 28; rehearsals and 109; template for 24–25
Untouchables, The 130
upstage 120
ura 9, 10, 61
Uses of Enchantment, The (Bettelheim) 47

Veep 176
verbs 145
Verdú, Maribel 135
View From the Bridge, A 74
violence: blocking the scene 131–133; emotional 161; in farce 159–161
vocal levels 150
Vogler, Christopher 22
vulnerability 109

Wall-E 75
Waller-Bridge, Phoebe 178
Wall Street 75
War and Peace 175
Warner Bros. 160
Washburn, Anna 177
Waters, John 164
Wayans, Damon 156
Wayne, John 10
Way of the Dragon 132
What the Butler Saw 165
When Harry Met Sally 75
Who, The 72
Who's Afraid of Virginia Woolf? 17, 73
Wiig, Kristen 136
Wilde, Oscar 129
Wild Strawberries 75
Williams, Hank 7
Williams, Tennessee 15
willing suspension of disbelief 86
Willis, Bruce 167
Wilson, August 11
Wilson, Rainn 159
Winfield, Jess 175
Wizard of Oz, The 10
wound 72, 73–74
writers: intentions 16–19, 38; working with 20–21, 105–106
Writers Guild of America (WGA) 30n5

Young Frankenstein 161, 168
Y Tu Mamá También 135

Zurer, Ayelet 136

Printed in the United States
by Baker & Taylor Publisher Services